Elín Jakobsdóttir

In the First Place

KERBER ART

Búrfell 1970
Foto/photo: Jakob Jakobsson

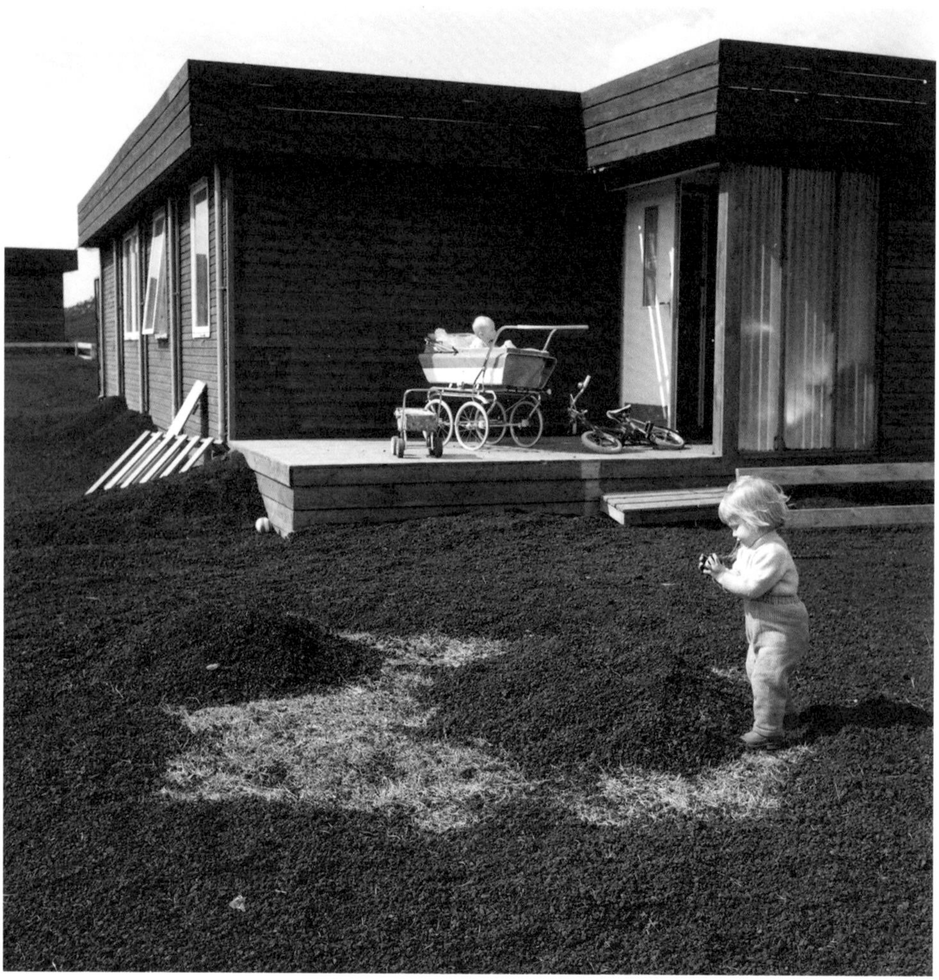

Zum Bildursprung zurück

Christine Nippe

Elín Jakobsdóttir und ich lernten uns 2006 in Berlin kennen und ich stellte ihre Arbeiten in zwei meiner Ausstellungen *Place Makers* (2007) und *Folding Unfolding Space* (2014) aus. In ihren Gemälden, Filmen, Zeichnungen und Skulpturen interessiert sich die Künstlerin für die Verbindung zwischen Imagination, Bildproduktion, Subjektivität und dem Körper. Ihre translokalen Bezüge zu Island, Schottland und Berlin spiegeln nicht nur diese unterschiedlichen Orte wider, sondern machen auch die Tiefe ihrer Arbeit aus. Ihr Oeuvre zeichnet sich durch eine ruhige und doch starke Intensität mit Verweisen auf das Unbewusste aus.

Die Einzelausstellung von Elín Jakobsdóttir in der Schwartzschen Villa trägt den Titel *In the First Place*. Jakobsdóttirs Wege durch Malerei und Film führen sie zurück zu einem Ort der Ursprünge im künstlerischen und geographischen Sinne. Von „dem ersten Ort" zu sprechen, bedeutet, einen ursprünglichen Ort zu evozieren, einen Ort des Beginns. Der Anfang eines Gedankens, der erste Akt. Ein Baby öffnet seine Augen und navigiert wortlos durch seine Umgebung. Vor diesem ersten Ort gab es kein „Wo", keine Vergangenheit, nichts zu sehen oder zu wissen. Nach diesem ersten Ort wird jedes und jedes andere Wo kommen.

Bei Elín Jakobsdóttir ist dieser erste Ort festgefroren in einer alten Schwarz-Weiß-Fotografie aus ihrer Kindheit: Sie zeigt die Künstlerin als kleines Mädchen kurz nach einer Eruption des Vulkans Hekla 1970 ganz in der Nähe ihres Hauses in Island. Das Bild wurde in Burfell, Südisland, aufgenommen, als die Künstlerin noch ein Kleinkind war. Auf dem Bild ist das Familienhaus zu sehen, das als Unterkunft für das Personal diente, das am Bau des nahegelegenen Wasserkraftwerks arbeitete. Zu sehen ist der Garten, der über und über von Bimssteinasche vom massiven Ausbruch des Vulkans Hekla bedeckt ist. Die Künstlerin zu diesem Ereignis: „Ich habe keine aktive Erinnerung daran, aber ich denke, dass diese Erfahrung mich geprägt haben muss, denn die amorphe, poröse Natur des schwarzen Bimssteins ist eine Qualität, die bis heute in meiner Arbeit zu sehen ist. Das Foto zeigt mich, wie ich den Bimsstein hochhalte und in ihn hineinstarre."[1]

1 Interview mit Elín Jakobsdóttir am 16.2.2021.

Die ungezügelten Kräfte der Natur haben sich tief in die Erfahrung von Elín Jakobdóttir eingeschrieben und finden in ihrer Kunst als *débordement* Ausdruck. Jakobsdóttir fasst diesen Moment in einem unserer Gespräche auf ihre Weise: „Dieses Konzept kommt sowohl in der Malerei als auch in den Filmen vor. In den Gemälden ist es einfach die Liquidität von Materialschichten, die die ursprüngliche Zeichnung stören und ein Chaos in den Produktionsprozess einbringen. Es ist das Konzept, das die Filme und Gemälde verbindet, ja es ist von den Gemälden aus in die Filme eingegangen, als Werkzeug, um den narrativen Fluss des Films zu unterlaufen und ein elliptisches Zeitergebnis zu schaffen, das die ‚kontinuierliche Gegenwärtigkeit' der Zeit in der Malerei widerspiegelt. Aber sagen wir, diese Diskussion bleibt immer innerhalb eines poetischen Territoriums. Es ist eine subversive Geste gegen die Vorherrschaft des Rationalen. Es geht um den Fluss der Ideen, ich würde sogar so weit gehen, es einen alchemistischen Überfluss zu nennen. Die Idee, dass das Unbewusste nicht durch das Rationale eingedämmt werden kann. Ein freudiger apokalyptischer Widerspruch." Den Moment des débordement bei Jakobsdóttir beschreibt die Kuratorin Henriette Huldisch wie folgt: „In broader terms, she evokes what she thinks of as the more fluid world of the mind that contrasts with the hard lines and edges of the world around us."[2]

2 Henriette Huldisch „Hinges Between Days", in: Elín Jakobsdóttir „Hinges Between Days", Edinburgh 2010, S. 3.

Elín Jakobsdóttirs Filme sind Meditationen zur menschlichen Wahrnehmung. Oftmals erforschen sie das Unterbewusste oder beinhalten traumähnliche Sequenzen. So auch in ihrem neuesten Film, den sie mit einer Super-8-Kamera in Glasgow und an der Südküste Islands im Corona-Sommer 2020 drehte. Der Film beginnt in Glasgow: ein kleiner Junge malt eine Figur mit blauer Farbe auf eine Leinwand, rollt sich selbst in die Stoffhülle ein und spricht durch eine Fensterscheibe mit Gesichtern, die dort auftauchen.

In dem an der Südküste Islands gedrehten Film sind Szenen mit isländischen Wildblumen, dem Strand von

Eyrarbakki und dem Meer zu sehen. Der Film setzt die Kunst in Beziehung zur Landschaft und konzentriert sich auf die Farben in der Natur. Ein weiteres Thema des Films ist die Abstammung und die Rolle der Frau. Der Film zeigt historische Fotografien von isländischen Frauen in traditioneller Kleidung neben den Werkzeugen, die sie benutzten. Ihre Präsenz zeigt sich im häuslichen Bereich.

Der Film setzt das Kunstwerk in Beziehung zu einem wichtigen kulturellen Ursprung des Ortes und zu einem Gefühl der Beständigkeit des Kunstwerkes im Laufe der Zeit. Der Film wurde am Standort des Læknishúsið aufgenommen, einem 1916 erbauten Betonhaus – eines der frühesten seiner Art in Island. Es folgt der Erfahrung eines kleinen Jungen in der Umgebung des Hauses und der Küstenlandschaft.

Hauptprotagonist des Filmes ist (wie bereits beschrieben) ein kleiner Junge, der in seinem Spiel mit der blauen Leinwand vertieft ist und diese in einer rätselhaften Choreographie aus den Fenstern des isländischen Hauses wirft, sie sich wie einen stillen Freund vor sich an den Tisch setzt und später mit ihr über die sommerlichen Blumenwiesen der Insel rennt. Der Film endet mit einer leicht melancholischen Sequenz: der Junge gibt den blauen Stoff den Gezeiten des Meeres preis. Fragen zur Kraft der Natur und der Vergänglichkeit des Lebens werden aufgeworfen.

Einer von Elín Jakobsdóttirs älteren Filmen *Worktable 1* S. 94
beginnt mit der Sicht auf den Hinterkopf eines kleinen Jungen. Indem die Künstlerin mit ihrer Kamera die Vogelperspektive einnimmt, befinden wir uns als Betrachter des Filmes in einer übergeordneten, beobachtenden Situation. Wir sehen, wie er mit Kohle eine Zeichnung anfertigt, die an einen Grundriss mit einem Treppenaufgang, Korridoren und Räumen erinnert. Gebannt verfolgen wir die in langen Einstellungen gefilmten Raumerkundungen des kleinen Jungen. Er vollendet die Zeichnung, näht einen Kragen für seine Mutter, spannt in sorgsamen Gesten Wollfäden in einem Spinnennetz um die Holzbeine eines Tisches, um schließlich die Innenräume der Wohnung durch das Treppenhaus zu verlassen. Wir tauchen in die Raumwahrnehmung einer anderen Zeit ein, erinnern uns an Höhlen, Baumhäuser, Verstecke unserer Kindheit.

Jakobsdóttir ist fasziniert von der Rolle der Erfahrungen für die Ausprägung innerer Bilder und wie diese Imaginationen in die Kunst einfließen. Ein Theoretiker, der sich mit diesen grundlegenden Gesetzen der Bildproduktion auseinandergesetzt hat, ist Hans Belting mit seiner Bildanthropologie. Belting spricht davon, dass der Körper Bilder produziere: „The exchange of experience for memory is an exchange between world and image. But the memory images that we thus acquire affect our every new perception of the world.“[3]

So würde unsere Erfahrung auch die Bilder der Welt immer wieder aufs Neue filtern, ist sich Jakobsdóttir sicher. Die Kunstproduktion käme damit einer Herstellung erster archetypischer Bilder aus den Tiefen des Gedächtnisses gleich.

Schaut man sich die verschiedenen Filme von Elín Jakobsdóttir an, so ist es wie ein Reigen sich wiederholender Traumbilder, die uns zum Beispiel in Form des Schlafsacks in einem ihrer frühesten Filme und in ihrem aktuellsten Film begegnet. Ihre amorphe Form fasziniert und wirft Fragen auf: Ist hier noch ein Mensch drin? Strahlt die Hülle noch die Wärme seines vorherigen Nutzers aus? Wem bietet der Stoff Schutz? Oder der kleine Junge mit seinen phantasievollen Raumentwürfen. Wer ist er? Und wofür steht er? Elín Jakobsdóttir entwirft magische Bilder, die uns immer wieder Rätsel aufgeben. Leise weben sie sich in unser Unterbewusstsein ein und leiten uns in die Zeit kindlicher Erinnerungen – an den Bildursprung zurück.

3 Hans Belting (2011), An Anthropology of Images', p. 44 Chapter 2.

Back to the Origin of the Image

Christine Nippe

Elín Jakobsdóttir and I met in Berlin in 2006, and I have presented her work in two of my exhibitions: *Place Makers* (2007) and *Folding Unfolding Space* (2014). In her paintings, films, drawings and sculptures, the artist is interested in the connection between imagination, subjectivity, the production of images and the body. Not only do her translocal links to Iceland, Scotland and Berlin reflect these different places, they also form the essence of her work's depth. Her oeuvre is distinguished by a calm and nonetheless powerful intensity featuring allusions to the unconscious.

Jakobsdóttir's solo exhibition at the Schwartzsche Villa is entitled *In the First Place*. The artist's paths through painting and film lead her back to a place of origins in an artistic and geographic sense. To speak of 'the first place' means evoking a primordial place, a place of beginning – the start of a thought, the first act. A baby opens her eyes and navigates her surroundings without words. Before this first place there was no 'where', no past, nothing to see or to know. After this first place comes every thing and every other where.

In Jakobsdóttir's work, this first place has become frozen in an old black-and-white photograph from her childhood: it shows the artist as a little girl, shortly after the 1970 eruption of the volcano Hekla very close to her house in Iceland. The picture was taken at Búrfell, in South Iceland, when the artist was still a small child. In the photo, you can see the family home which provided the personnel working on the construction of the nearby hydroelectric power station with a place to live. The garden can be seen, covered by layer upon layer of volcanic ash from the massive eruption of the volcano Hekla. Regarding this event, the artist has said: "I have no active memory of it, but I think this experience must have deeply influenced me, because the amorphous, porous nature of the black pumice is a quality that can still be seen in my work today. The photo shows me holding up a piece of pumice and staring into it."[1]

1 Interview with Elín Jakobsdóttir on 16 February 2021.

This experience of the unbridled forces of nature etched itself deeply into the mind of Jakobsdóttir and finds expression in her art as *débordement*. During one of our conversations, Jakobsdóttir summarised this aspect in her own way: "This concept appears in both my painting and films. In the paintings it is simply the fluidity of the layers of material, which disrupt the original drawing and introduce chaos into the production process. This is the concept that links the films and paintings, indeed, it made its way into the films from the paintings – as a tool to undermine the narrative flow of the film and to create an elliptical temporal effect that reflects the 'continual present time' in painting. But let's say that this discussion always remains within a poetic territory. It is a subversive gesture against the dominance of the rational. It is about the flow of ideas; I would even go so far as to call it an alchemical overflowing. The idea that the unconscious cannot be contained through the rational. A joyous, apocalyptic contradiction." The curator Henriette Huldisch has described the aspect of *débordement* in Jakobsdóttir's work as follows: 'In broader terms, she evokes what she thinks of as the more fluid world of the mind that contrasts with the hard lines and edges of the world around us.'[2]

2 Henriette Huldisch, 'Hinges Between Days', in: Elín Jakobsdóttir, 'Hinges Between Days' (Edinburgh, 2010), p. 3.

Jakobsdóttir's films are meditations on human perception. They often explore the unconscious or contain dream-like sequences. This is also the case in her most recent film, which she shot with a Super8 camera in Glasgow and on the southern coast of Iceland in the Corona summer of 2020. The film begins in Glasgow: a little boy paints a figure on a canvas with blue paint, rolls himself up in the cloth covering and speaks through a window pane with faces that appear there.

In the film shot on the southern coast of Iceland, we see scenes featuring Icelandic wild flowers, the beach at Eyrarbakki and the sea. The film places art in connection with the landscape and concentrates on the colours found in nature. The descent and role of woman is another theme of the film. It shows historical photographs of Icelandic women in traditional dress alongside the tools that they used. Their presence shows itself in the domestic realm.

The film places the artwork in connection with an important cultural origin of this place and a feeling of the artwork's persistence over the course of time. It was shot at the site of the Læknishúsið, a concrete house constructed in 1916 as one of the first of its kind in Iceland. The film follows the experiences of a little boy in the area around the house and in the coastal landscape.

The film's main protagonist is (as previously described) a little boy who is absorbed in his play with the blue canvas and, in an enigmatic choreography, throws it out the windows of the Icelandic house, sets it in front of himself at the table like a silent friend, with whom he later runs across the summery, flower-filled Icelandic garden. The film ends with a slightly melancholic sequence: the boy turns the blue material over to the tides of the sea. Questions are raised about the power of nature and the transience of life.

Worktable 1, one of Jakobsdóttir's older films, begins p. 94 with a view of the back of a little boy's head. Because the artist has taken up a bird's-eye view with her camera, we find ourselves in a superior, observing situation as viewers of the film. We see how he uses charcoal to create a drawing reminiscent of a floor plan with stairs, corridors and rooms. Captivated, we follow the little boy's explorations of space, which are filmed in lengthy shots. He completes the drawing, sews a collar for his mother, stretches wool threads in a spiderweb around the wooden legs of a table by means of careful gestures and then finally exits the interior of the flat through the stairwell. We are immersed in the perception of space from another time: we recall caves, tree houses and hiding places from our childhood.

Jakobsdóttir is fascinated by the role of experiences in shaping our inner images and how these imaginations make their way into art. One theorist who has occupied himself with these fundamental laws of image production is Hans Belting, with his anthropology of images. Belting talks about the body producing images: 'The exchange of experience for memory is an exchange between world and image. But the memory images that we thus acquire affect our every new perception of the world.'[3] Jakobsdóttir feels certain

3 Hans Belting, *An Anthropology of Images* (Princeton, 2011), p. 44.

that our experience also repeatedly re-filters the images of the world. The production of art would thus be equivalent to creating the first archetypical images from the depths of our memory.

Looking at Jakobsdóttir's different films, they are like a round dance of repeating dream images that we encounter, for example, in the form of the sleeping bag in one of her earliest films and in her most recent film. Its amorphous form is fascinating and raises questions: Is there still a person in it? Is this covering still radiating the warmth of its previous user? Who is the material offering protection? Or the little boy with his imaginative designs for spaces: Who is he? And what does he stand for? Elín Jakobsdóttir sketches magical images that repeatedly present us with riddles. They quietly weave their way into our subconscious and lead us to the time of childhood memories – back to the origin of the image.

In the First Place
Super-8-Film auf 2K gescannt
Super8 film scanned to 2K
21 minutes, silent
2021

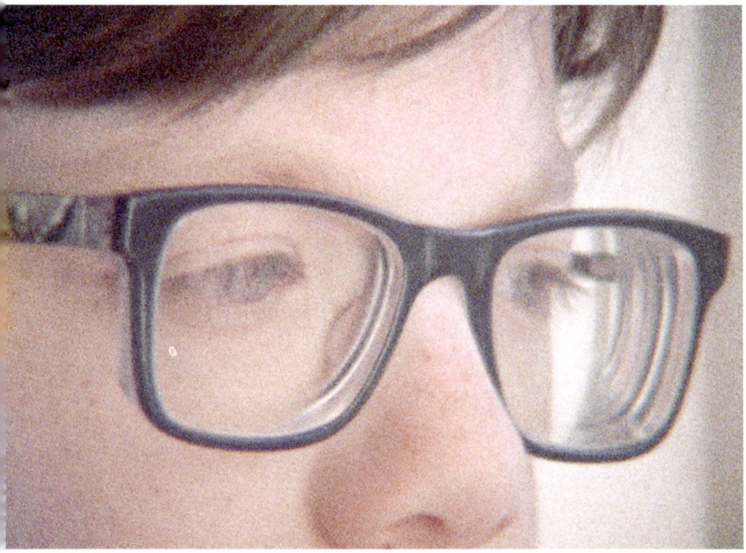

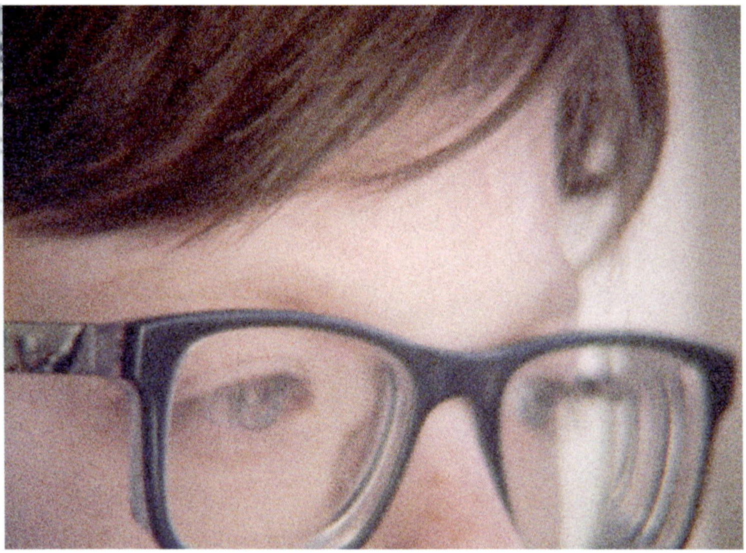

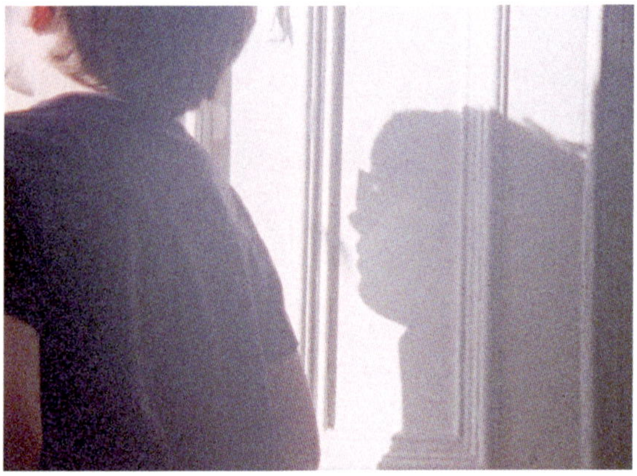

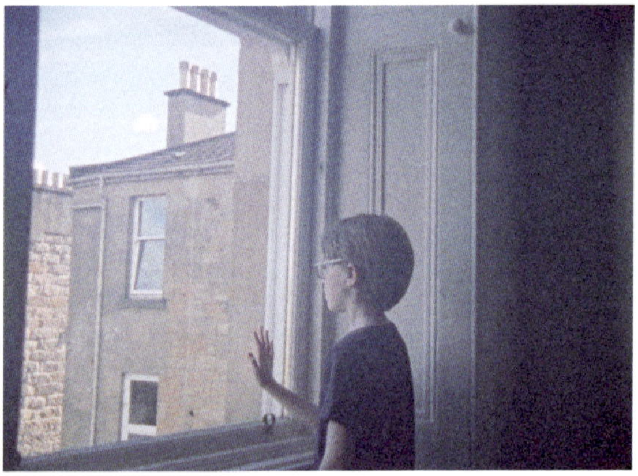

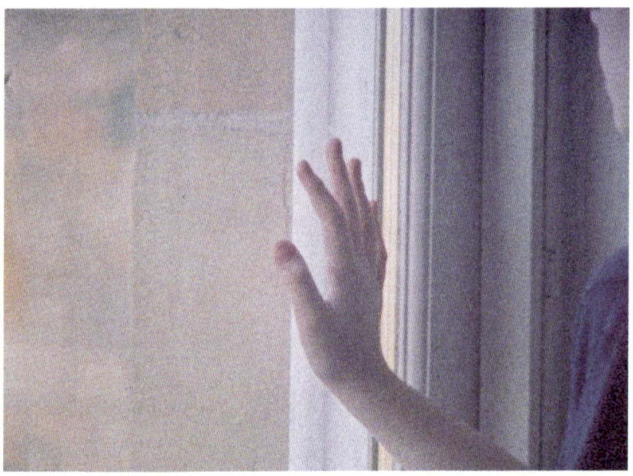

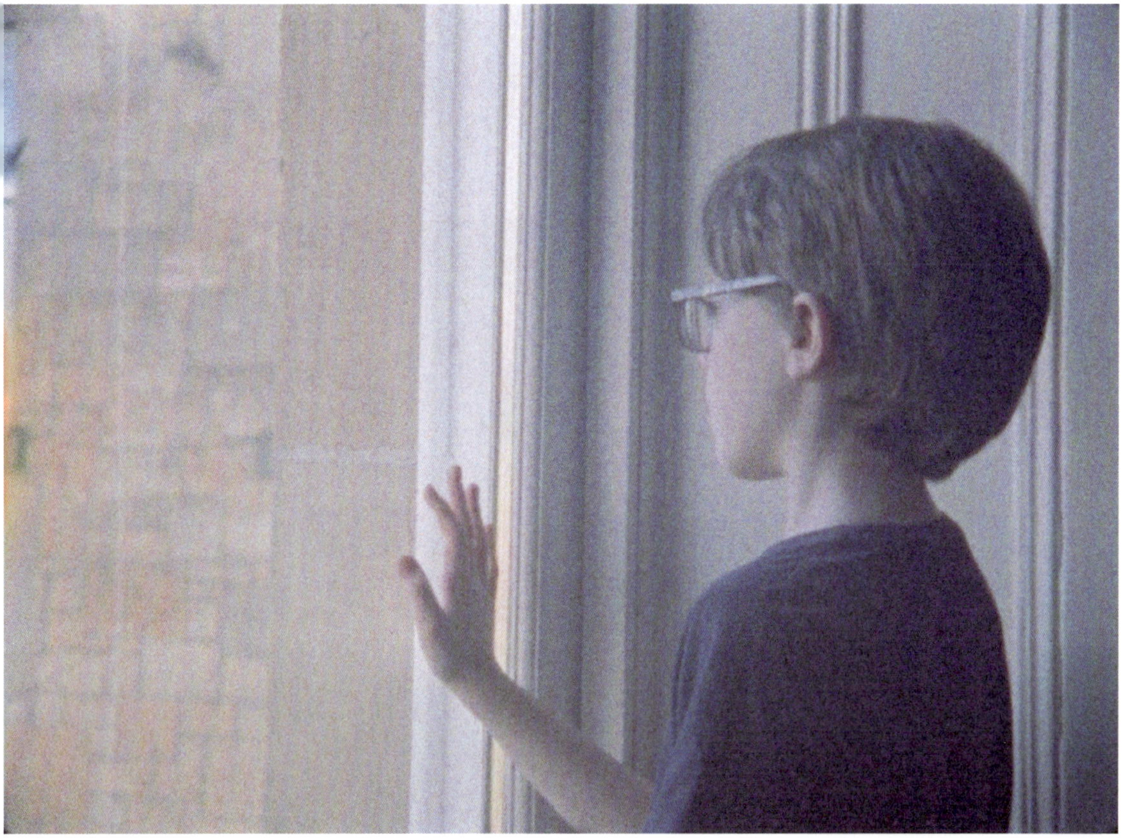

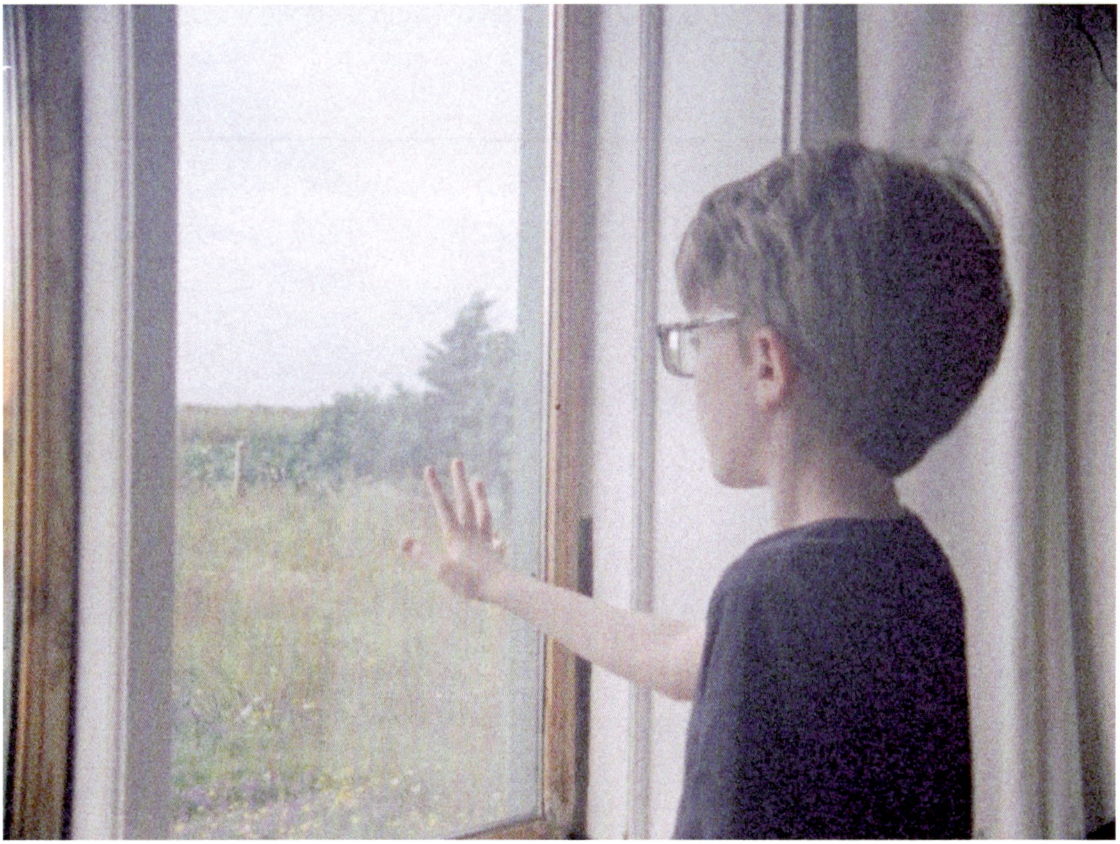

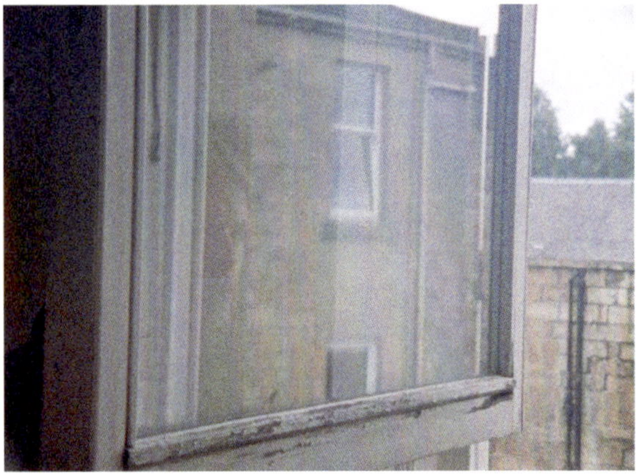
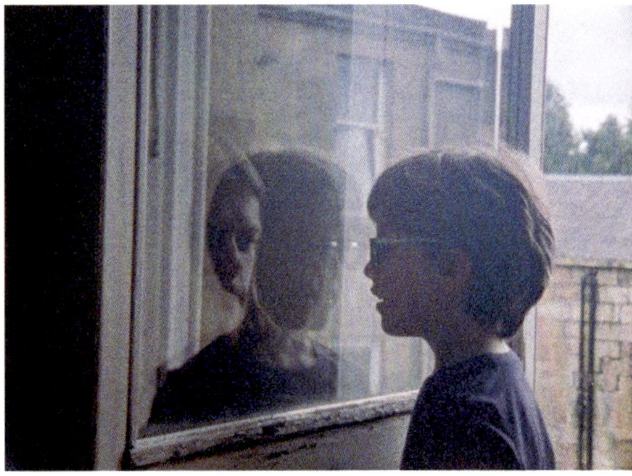
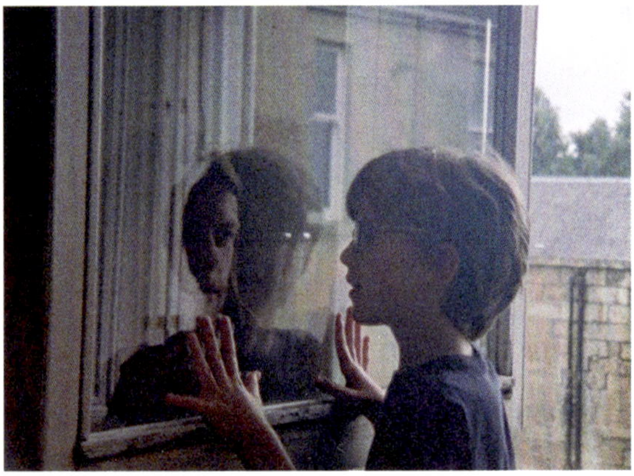
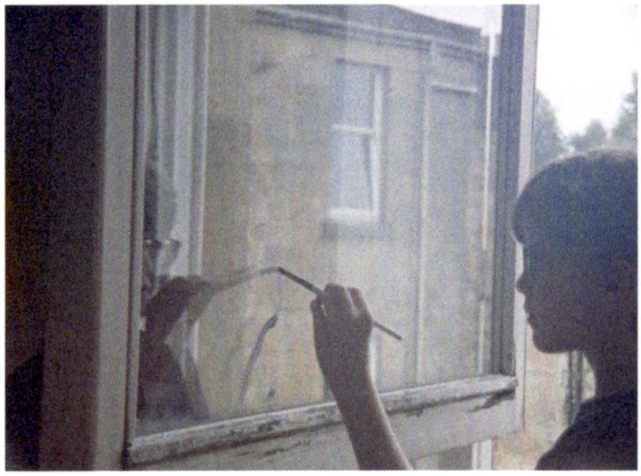
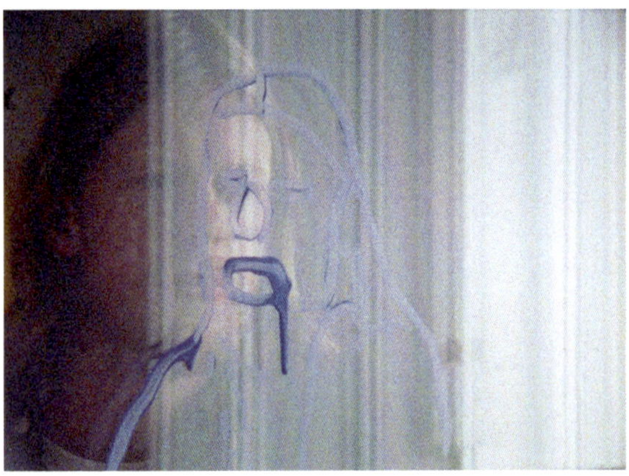
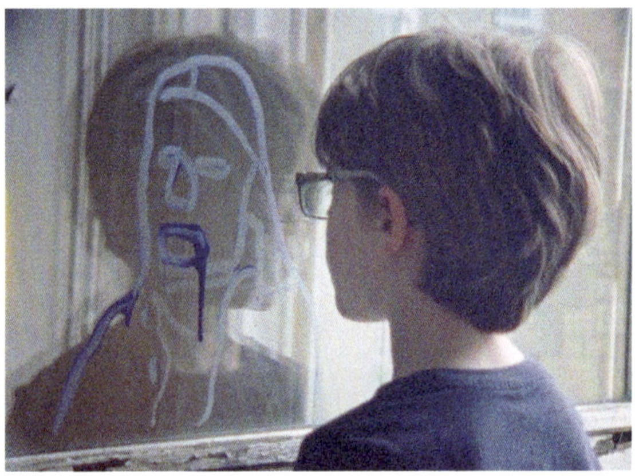

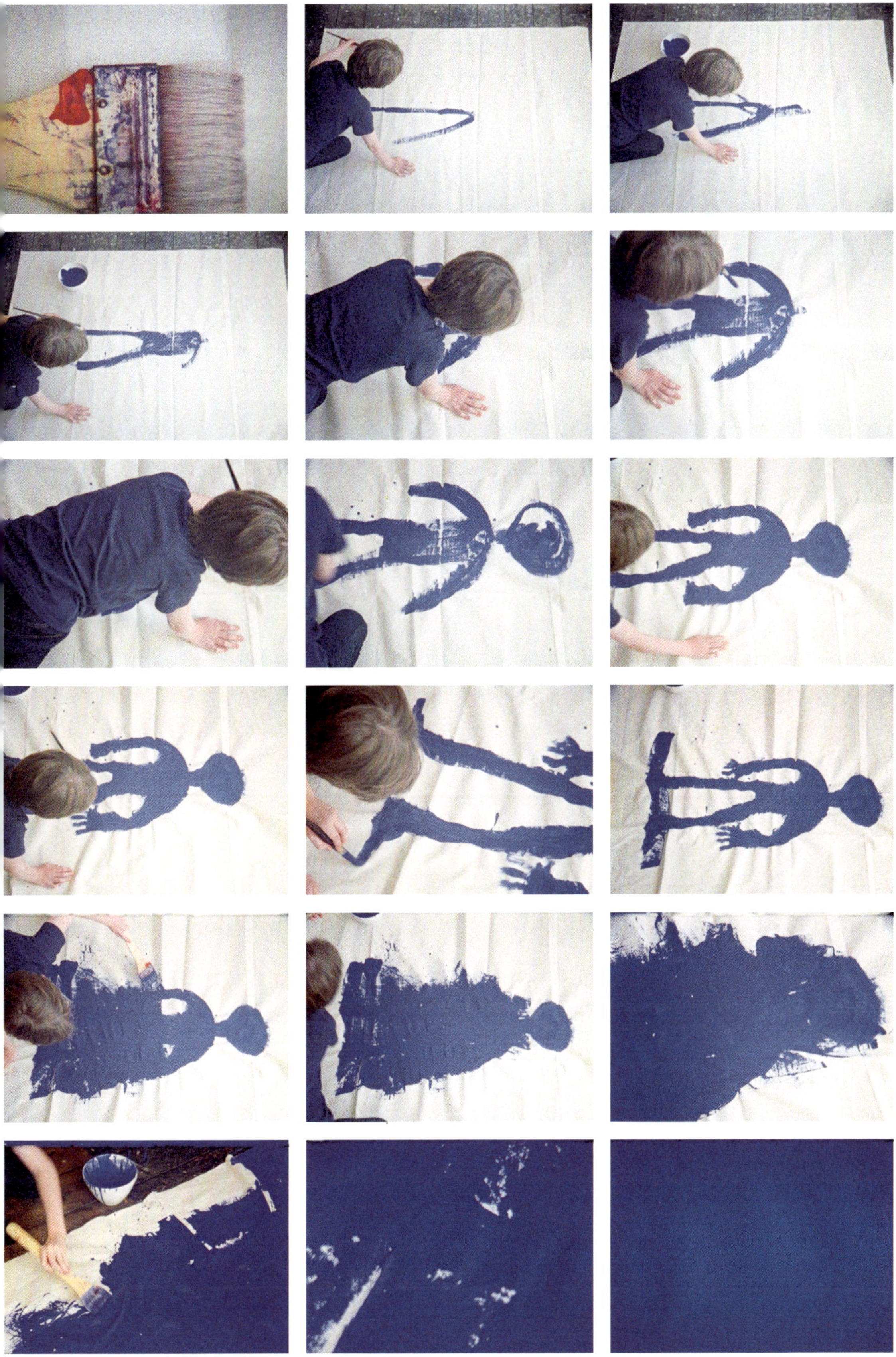

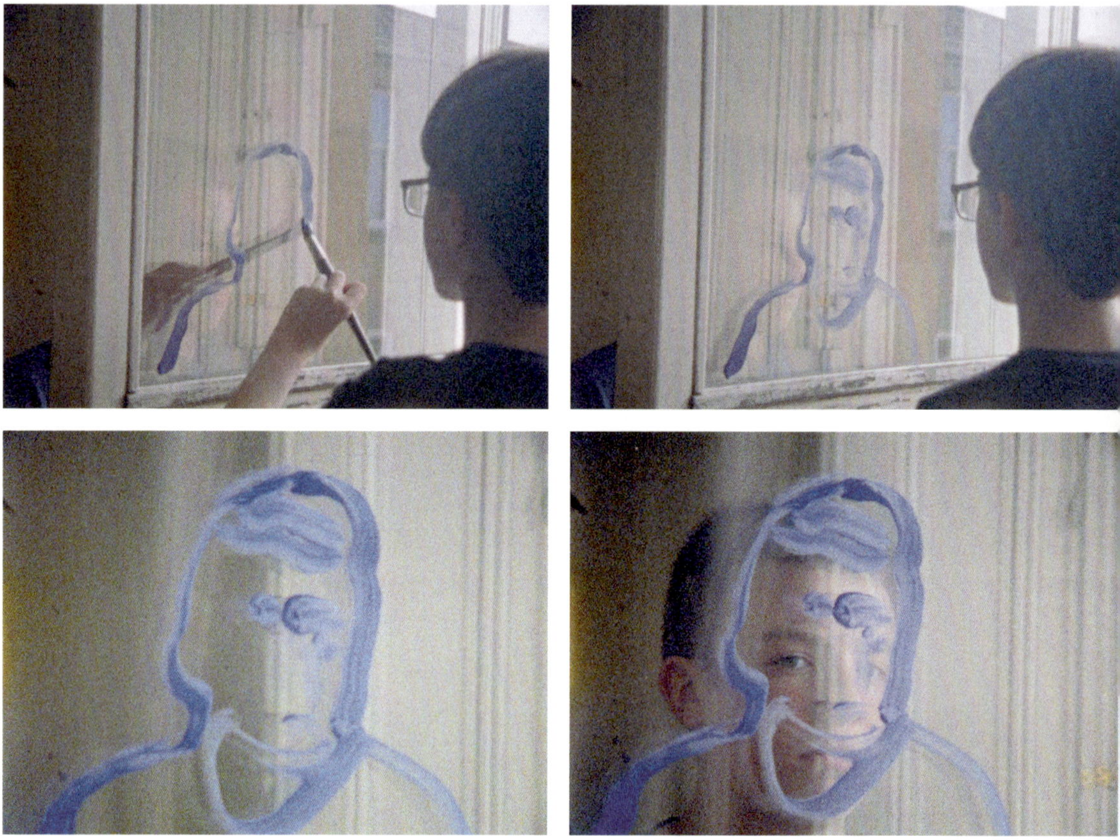

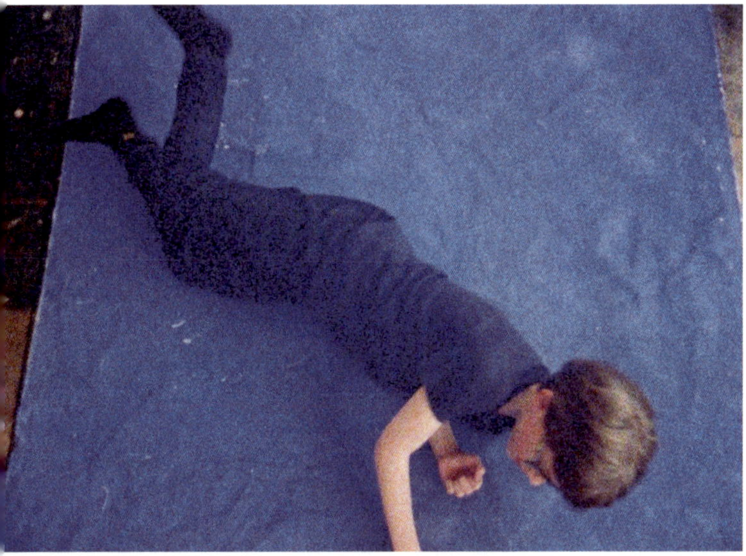

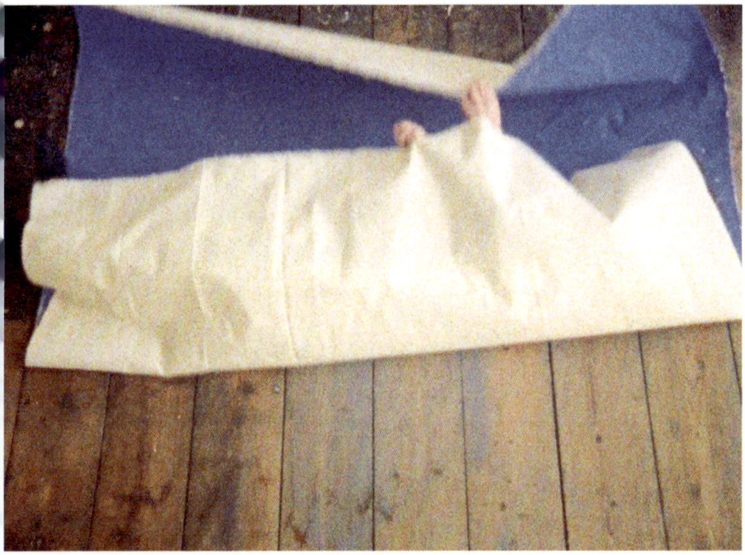

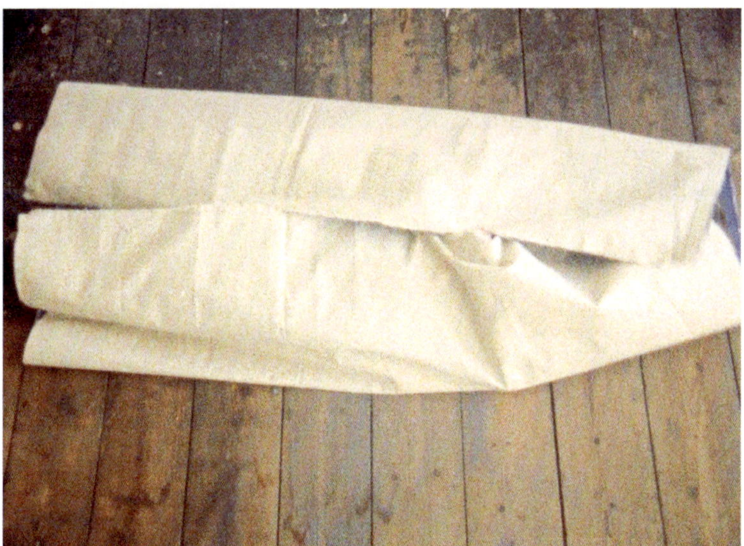

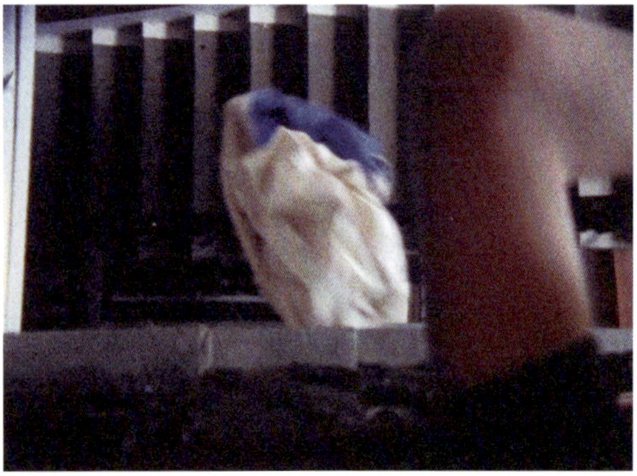
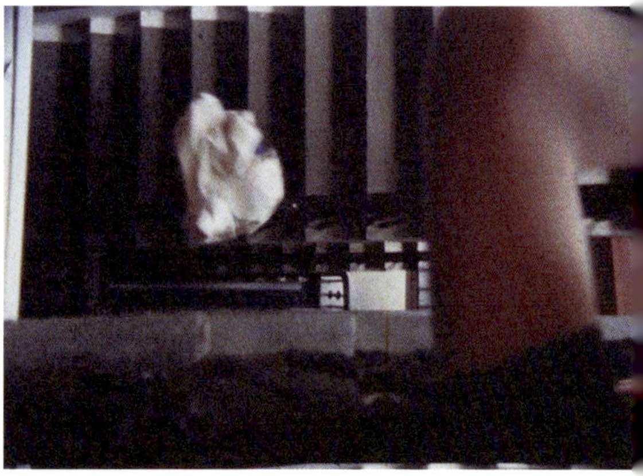
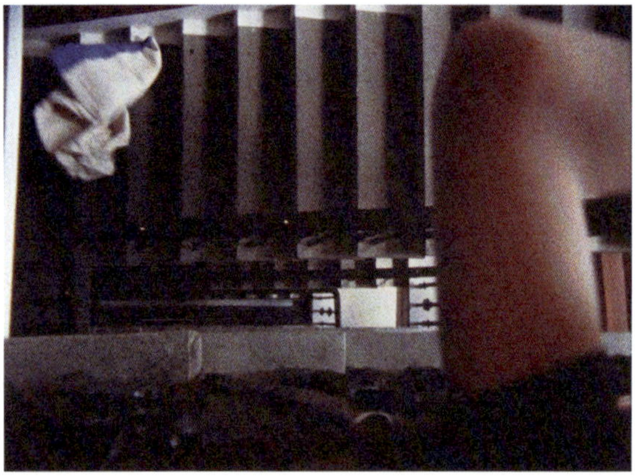
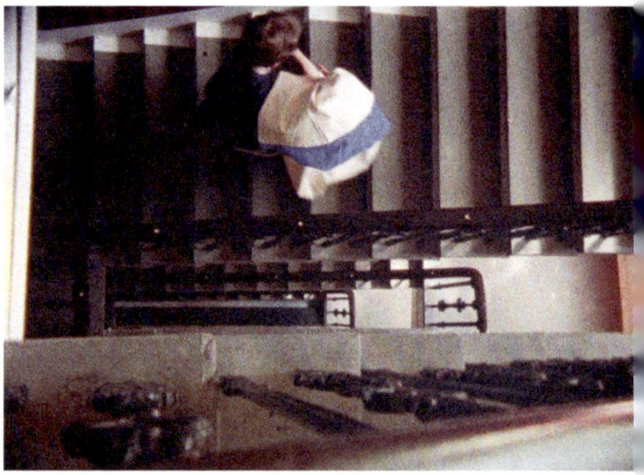
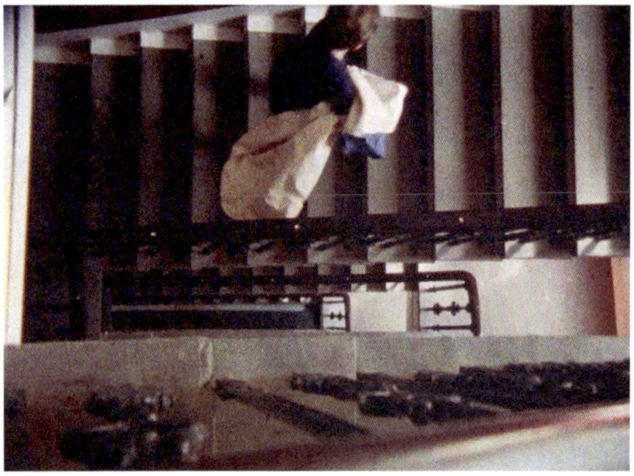
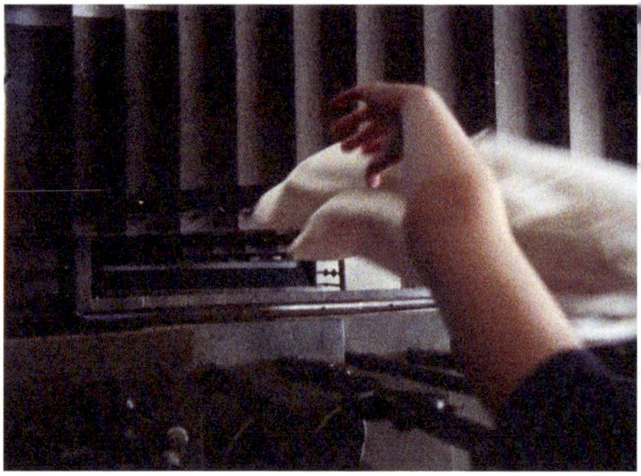
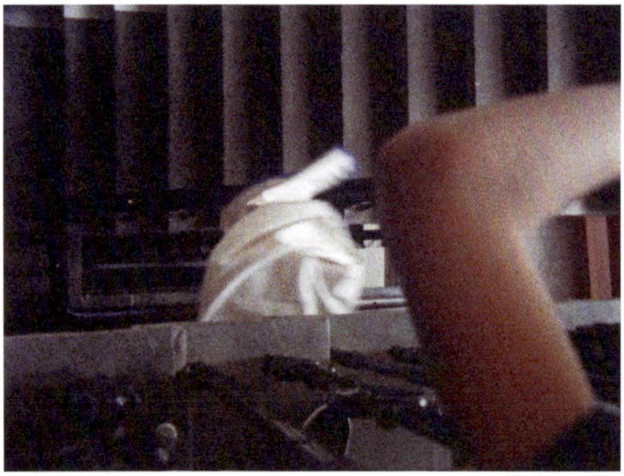
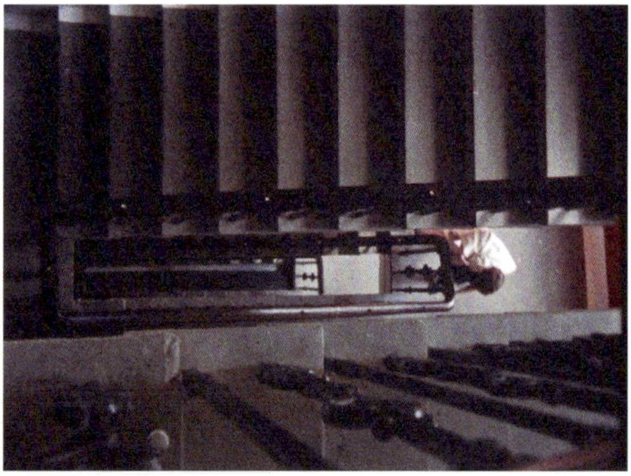

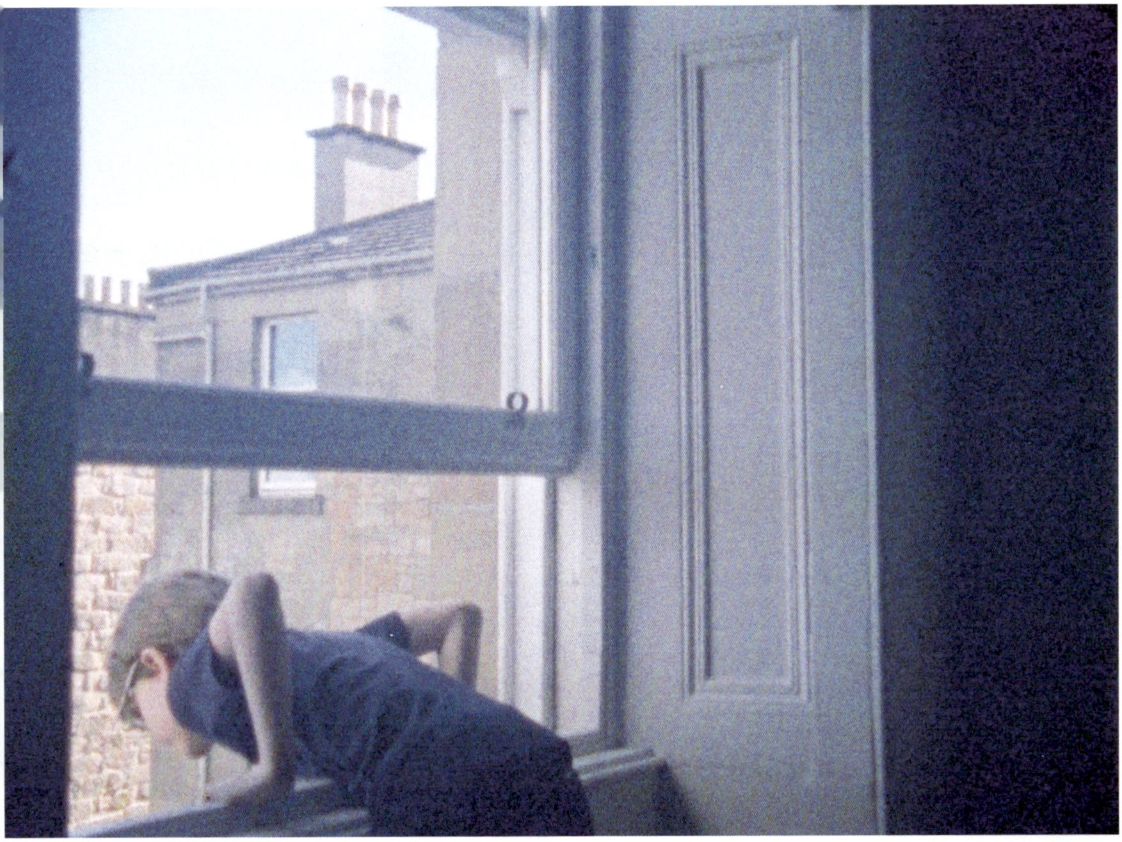

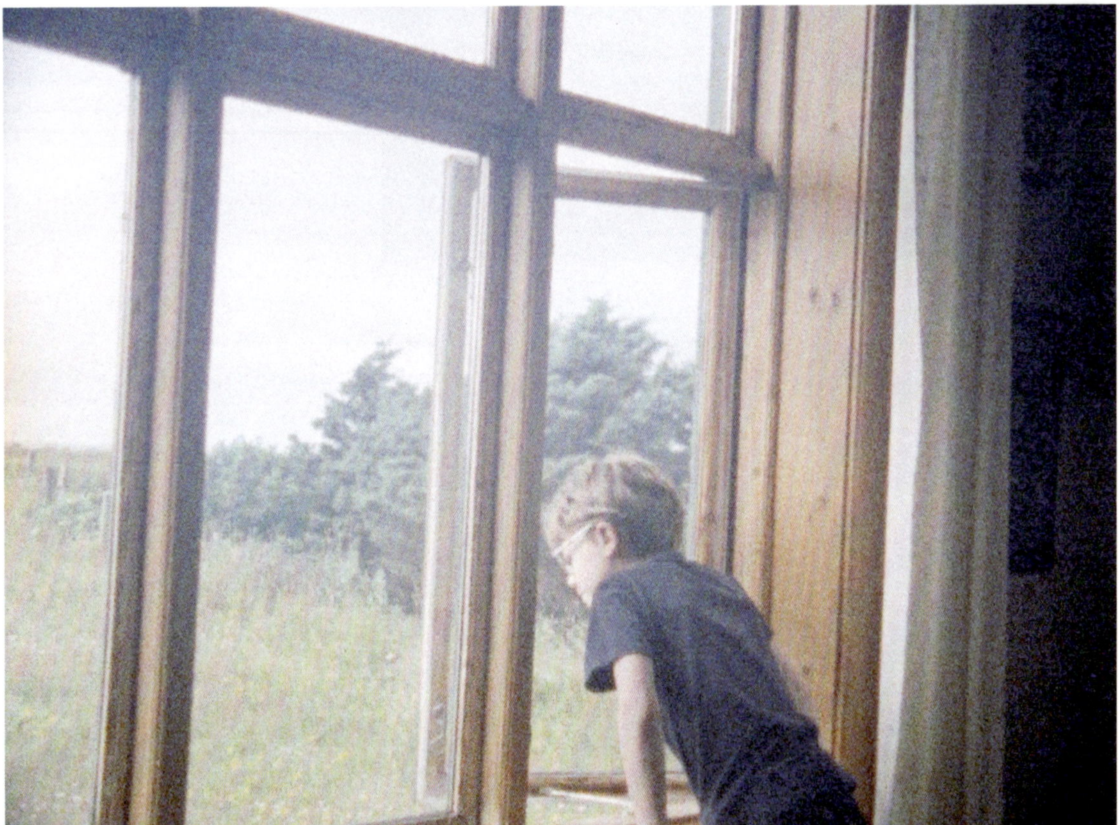

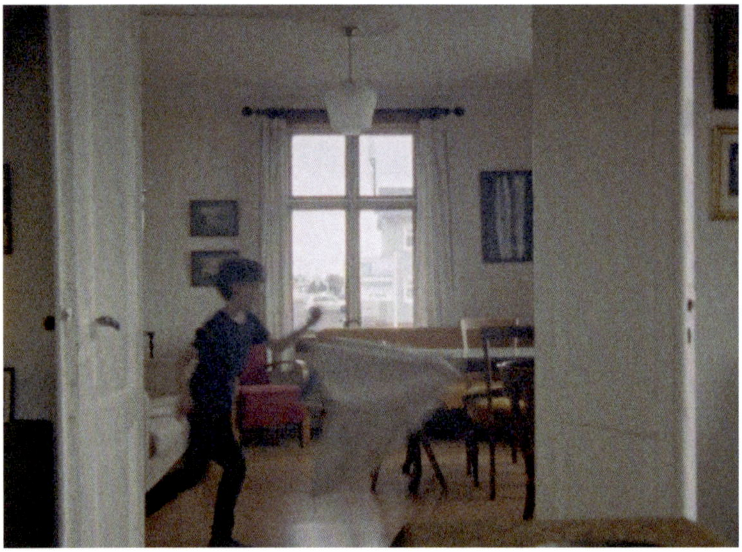

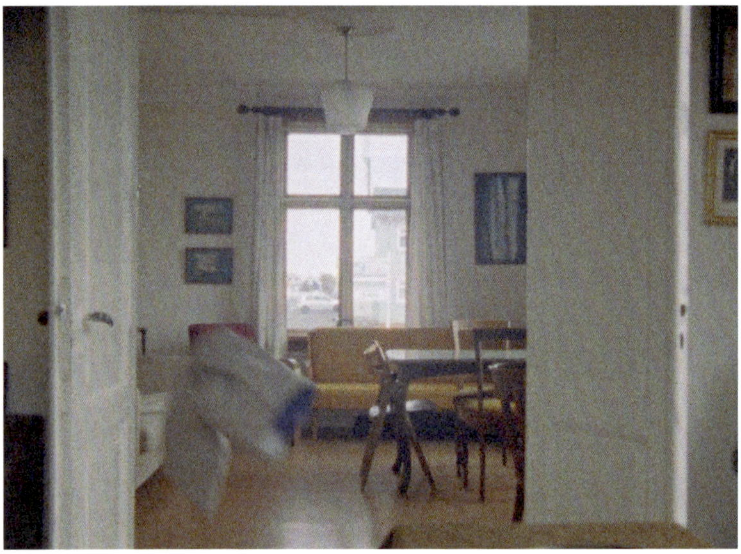

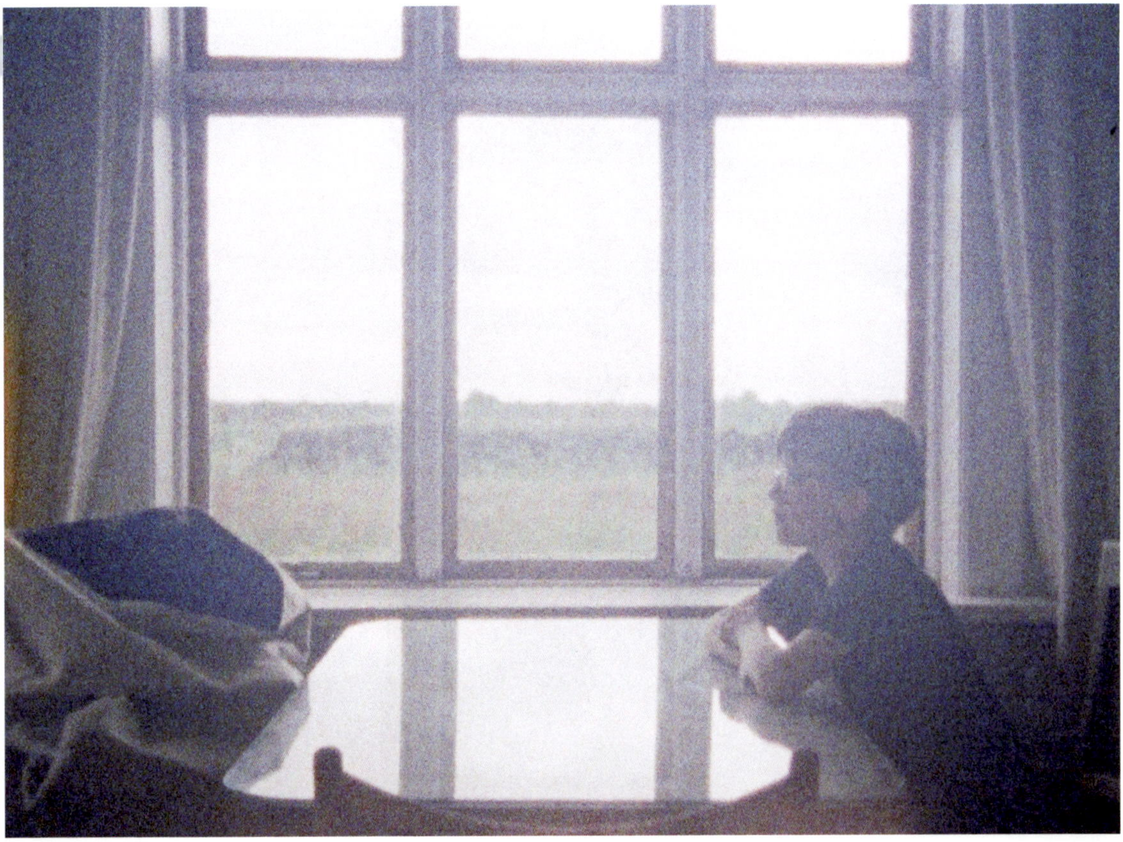

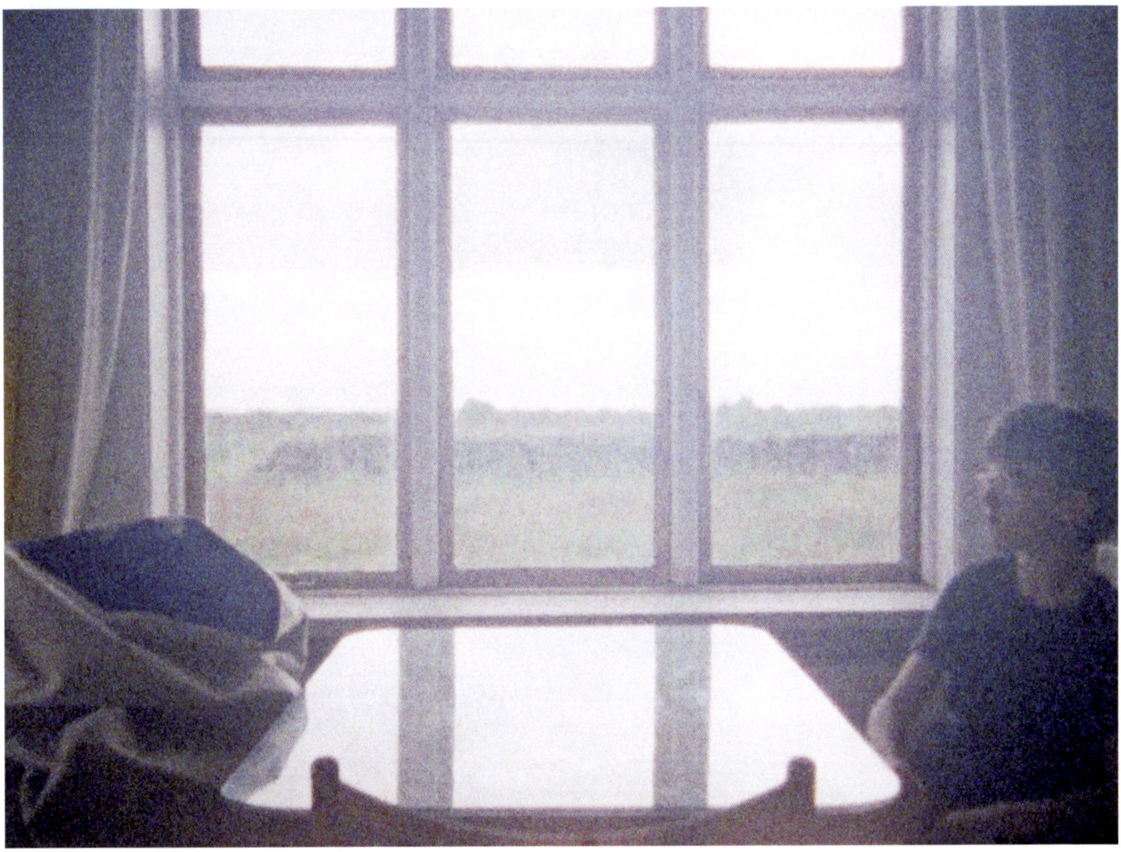

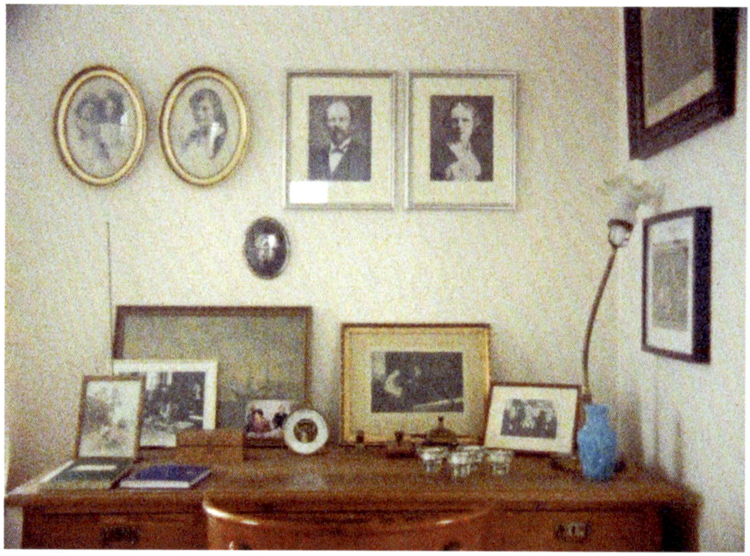

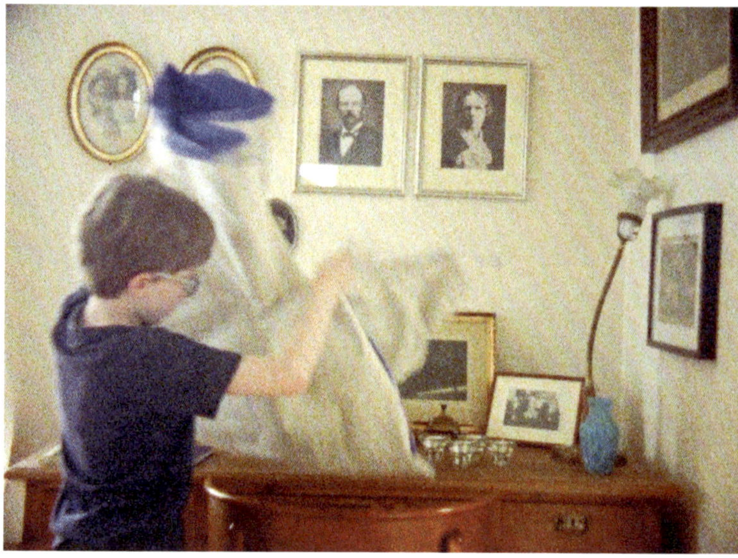

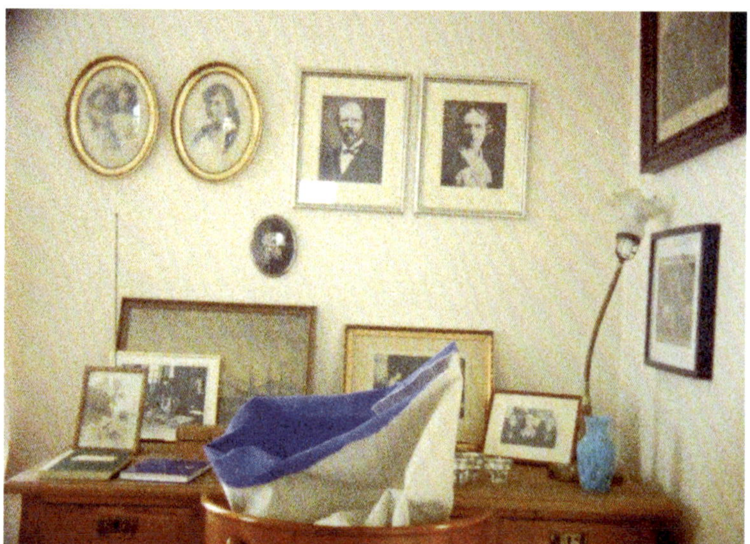

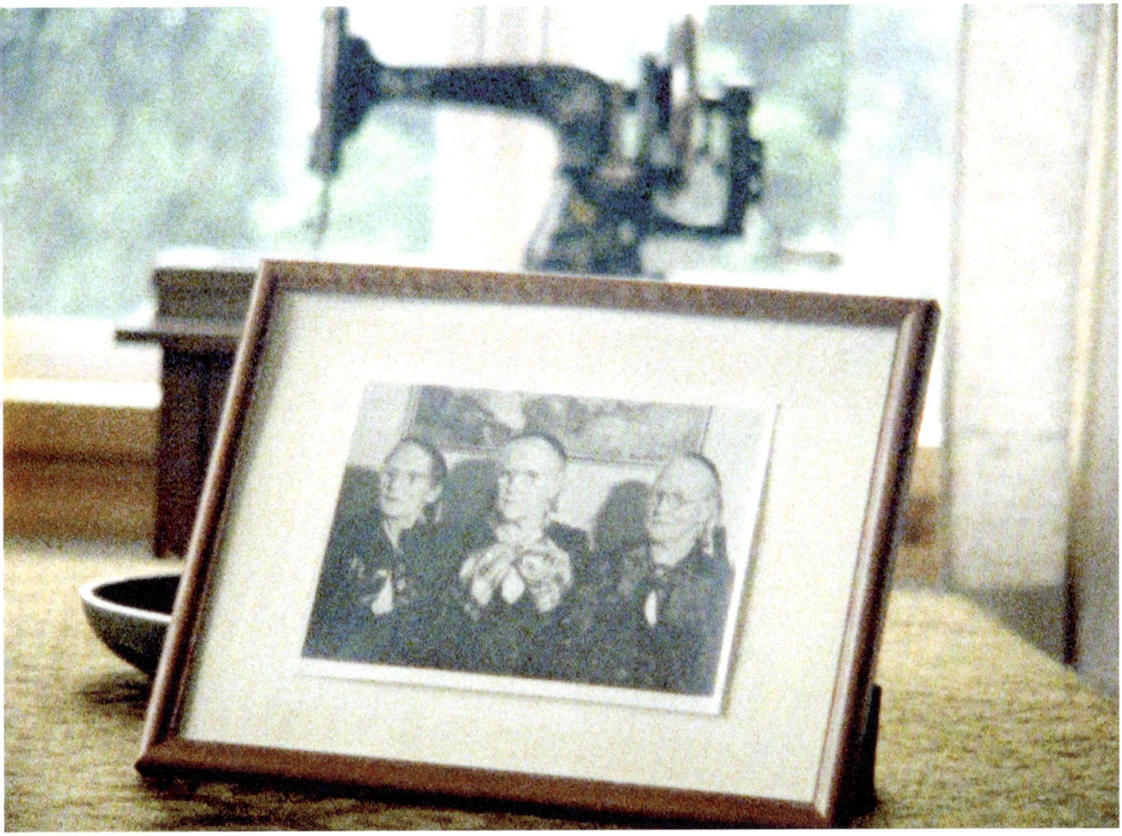

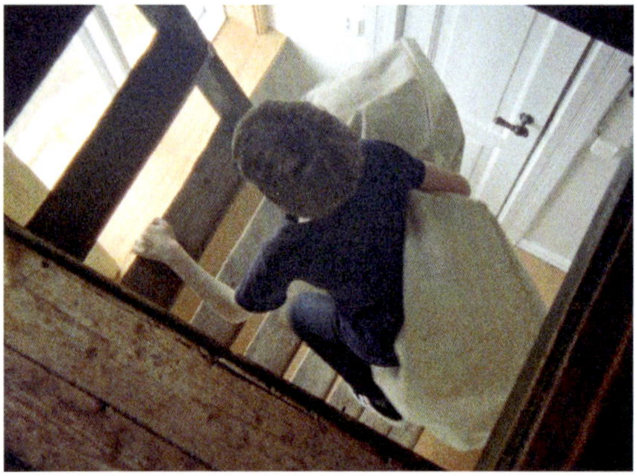
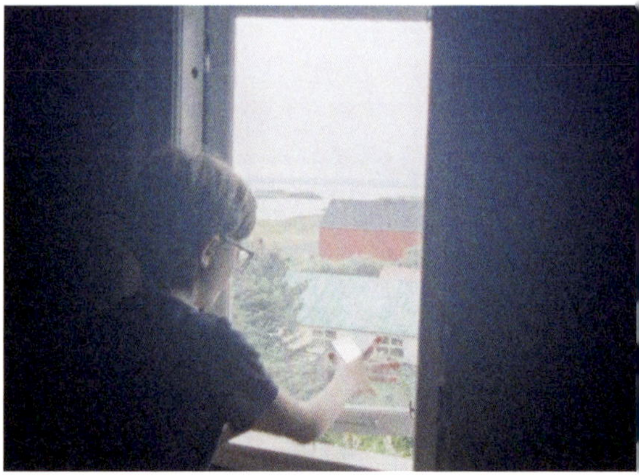
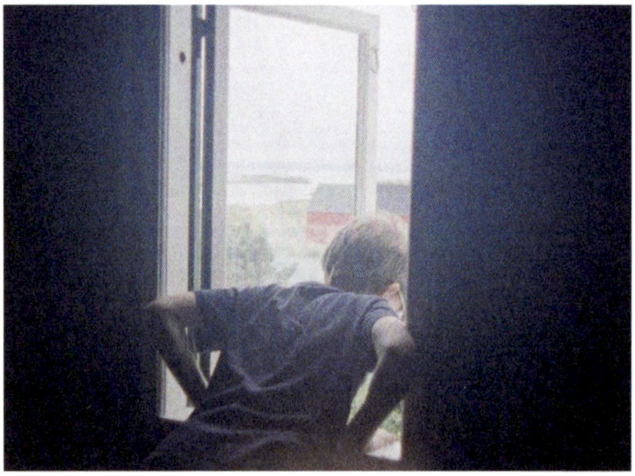
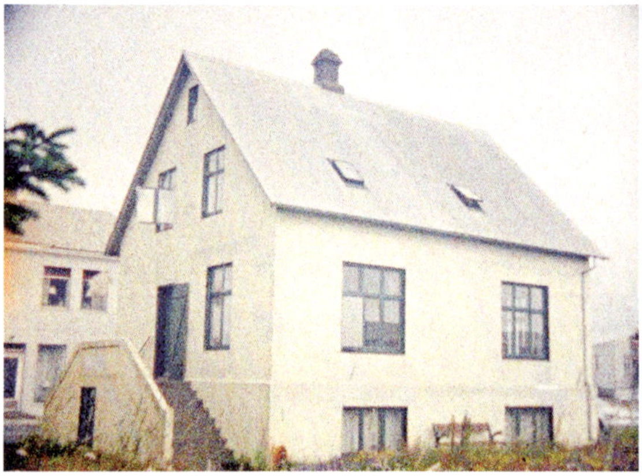
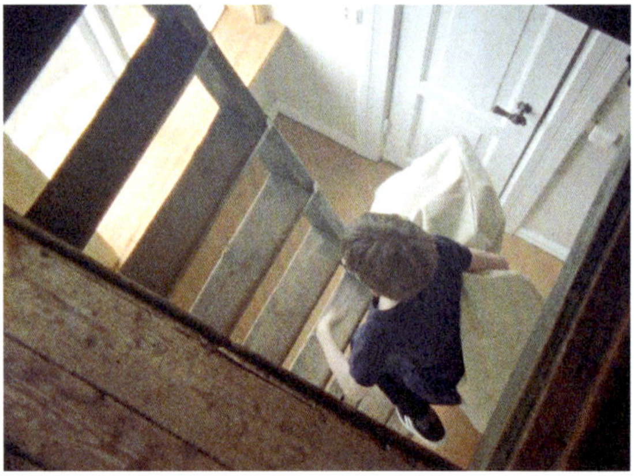
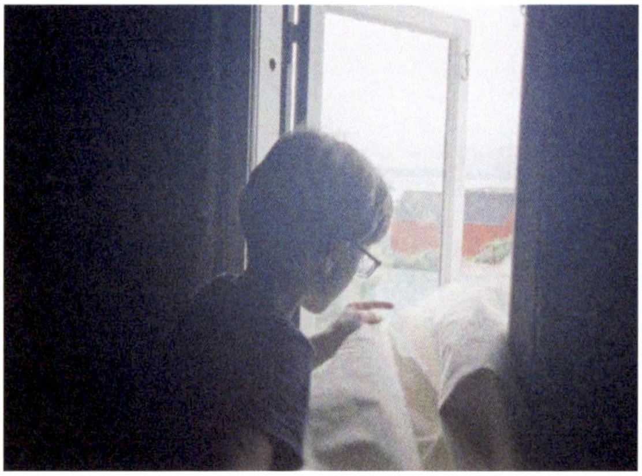
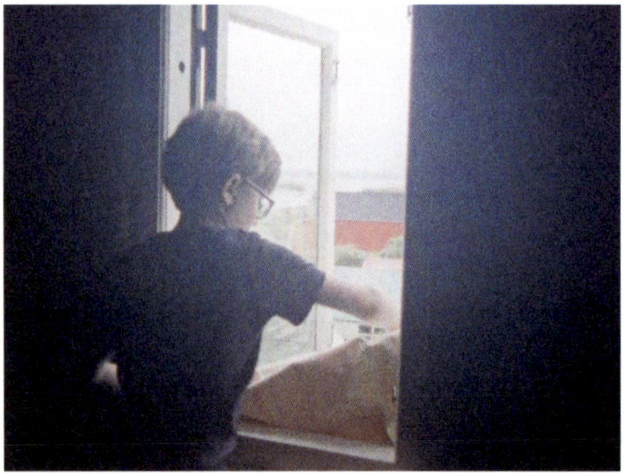
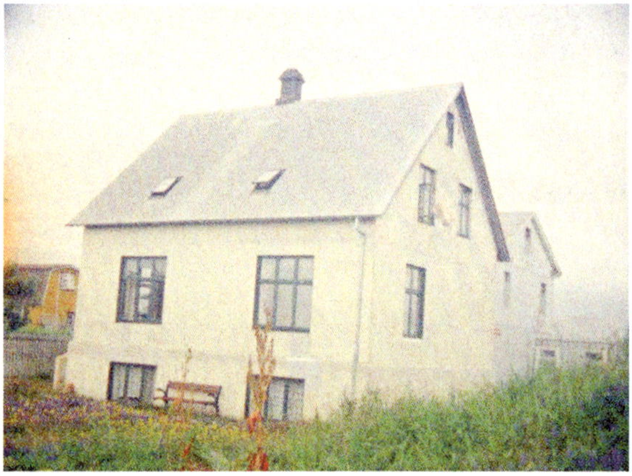

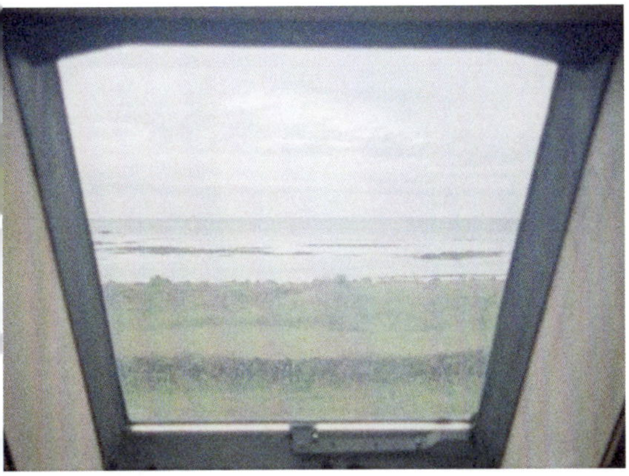

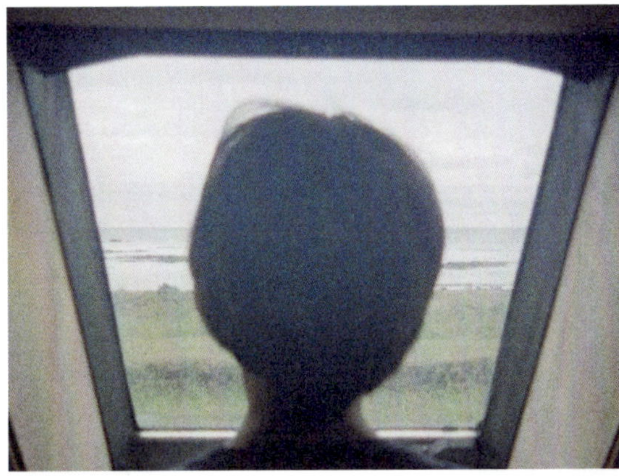

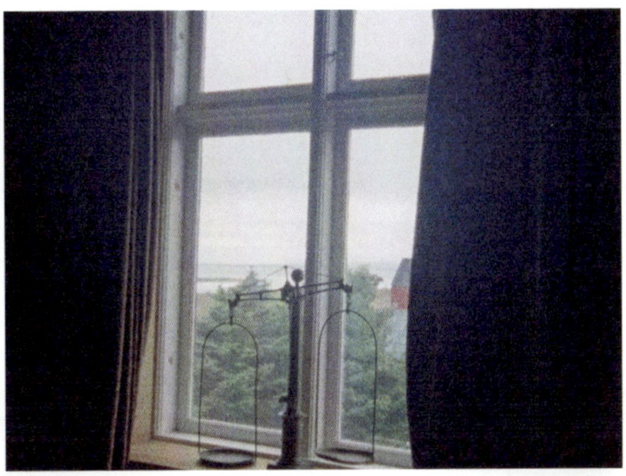

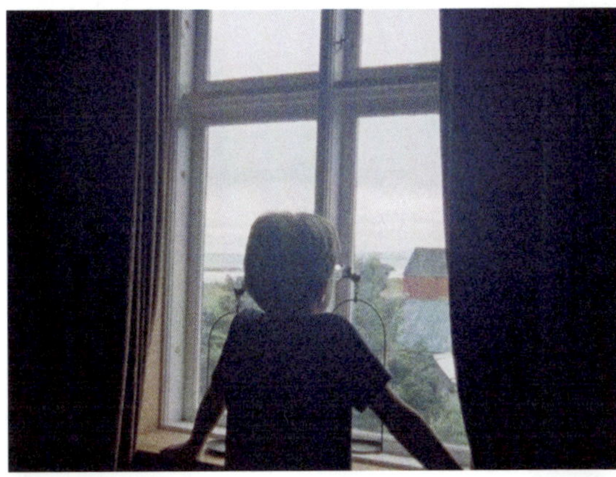

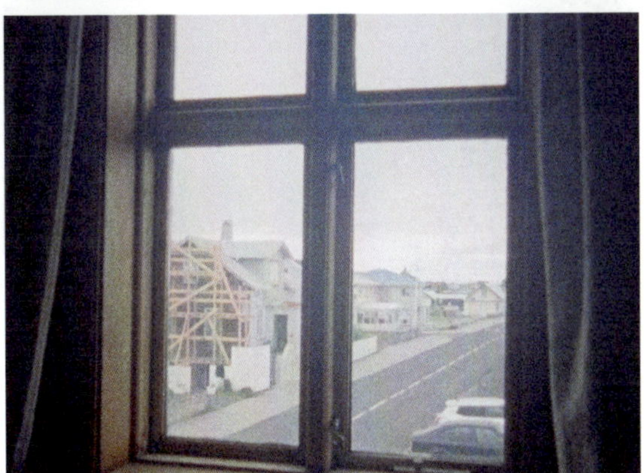

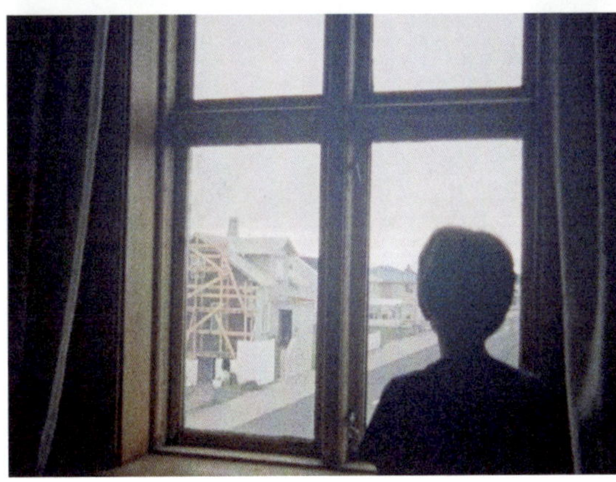

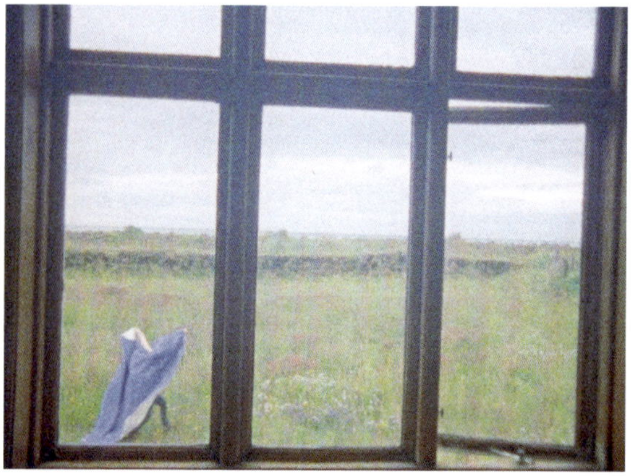
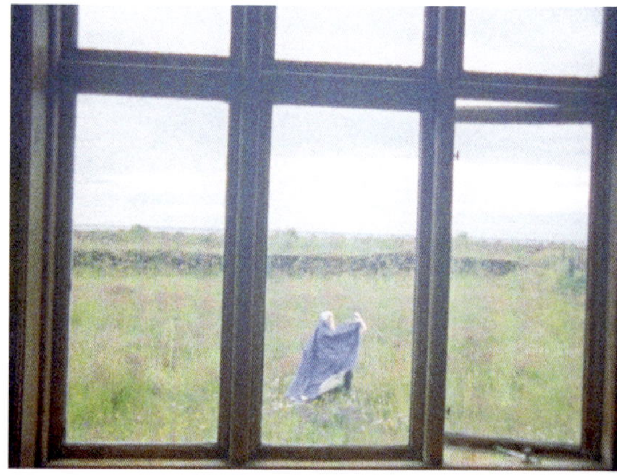
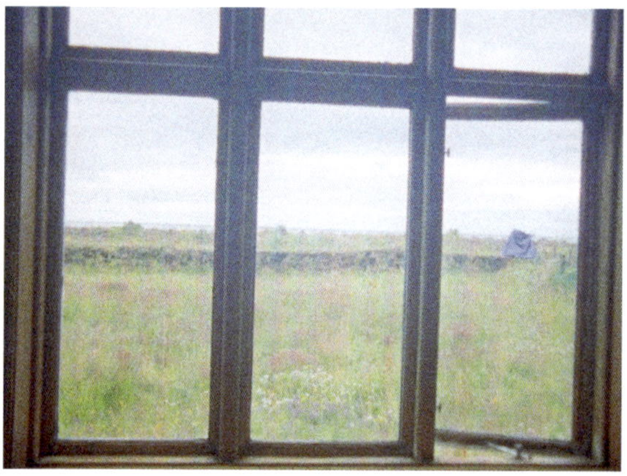
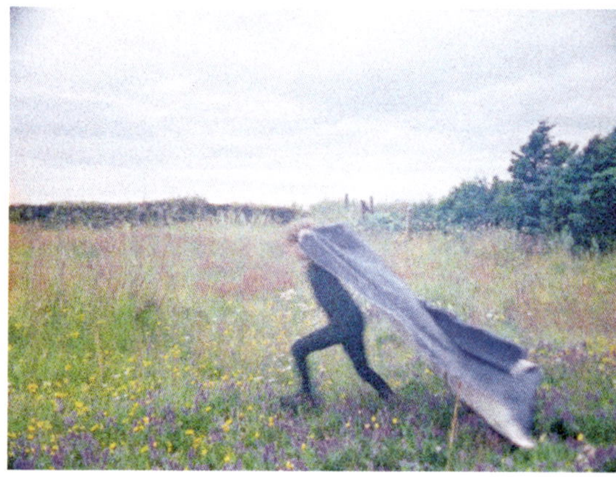
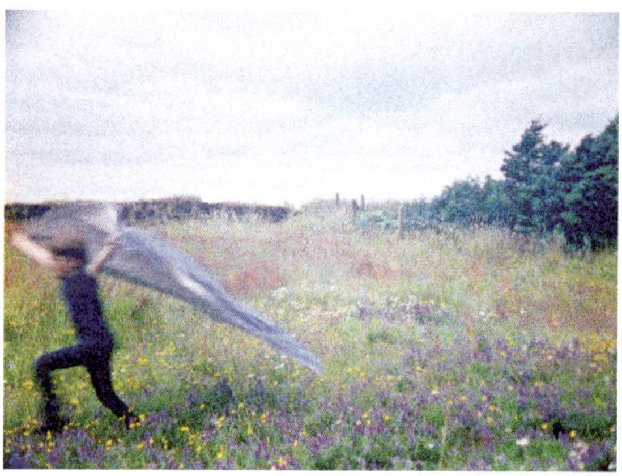
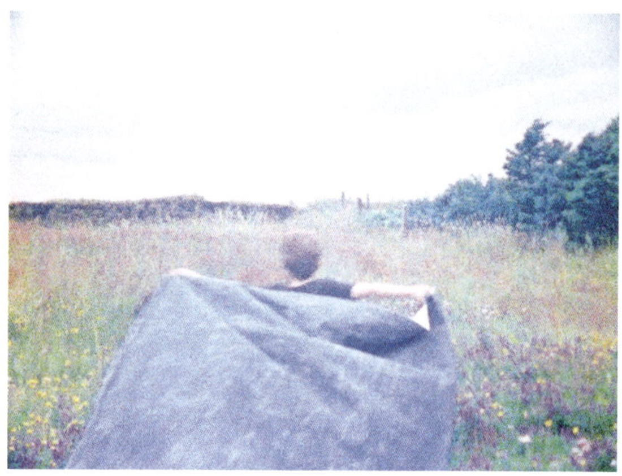
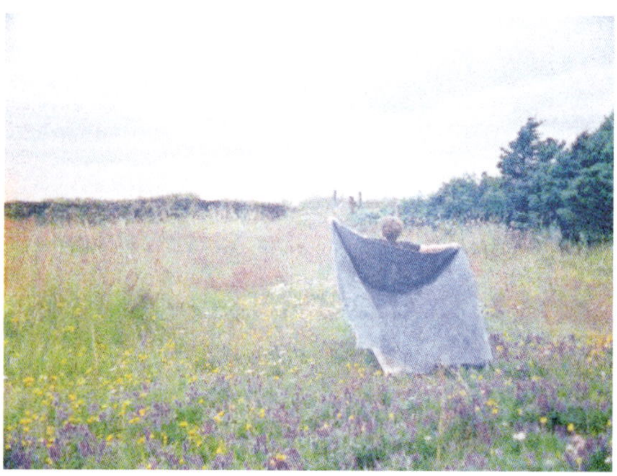
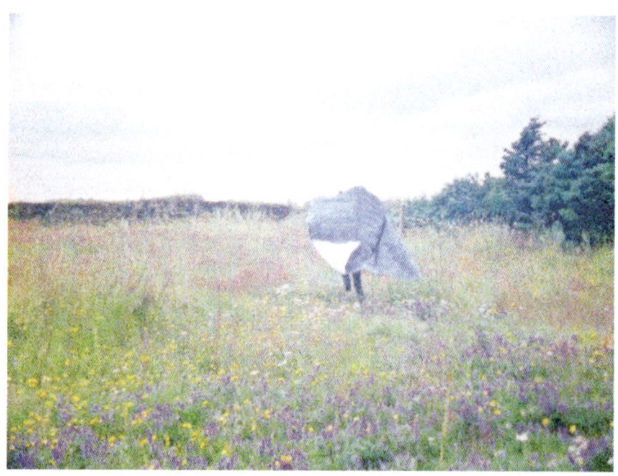

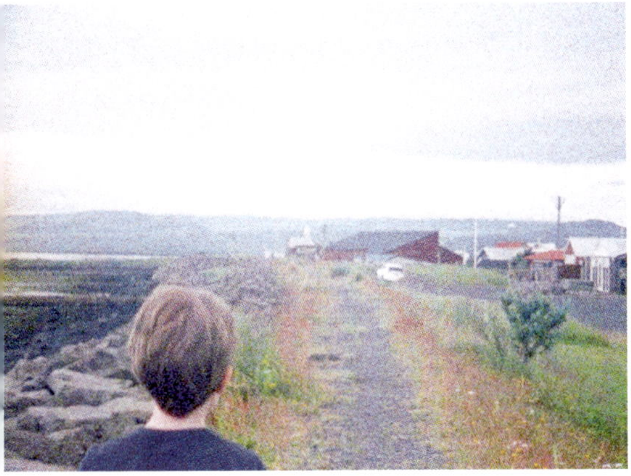
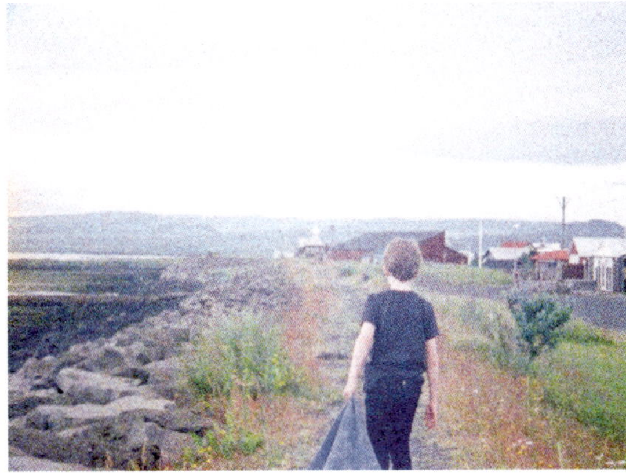
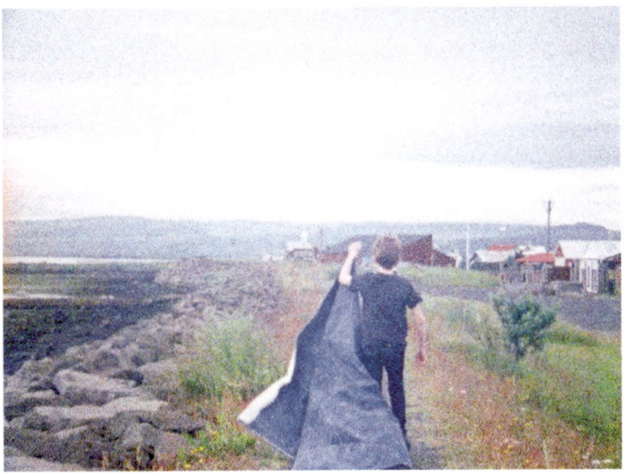
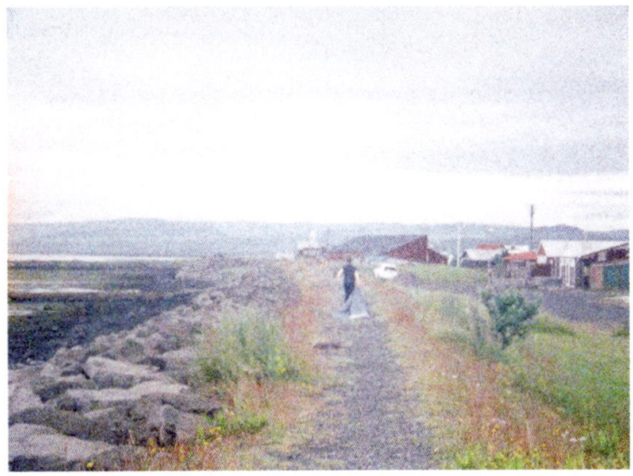

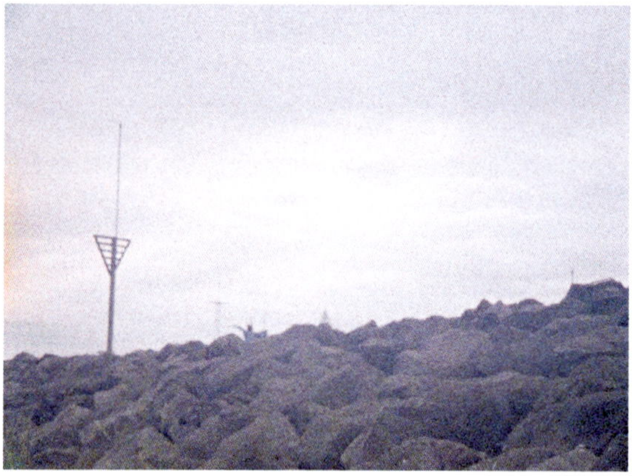
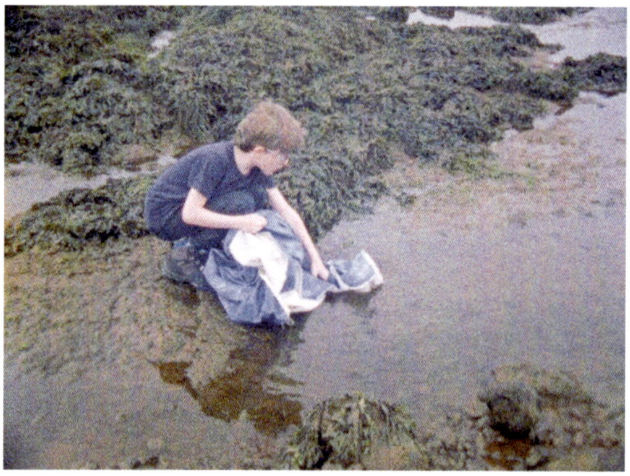
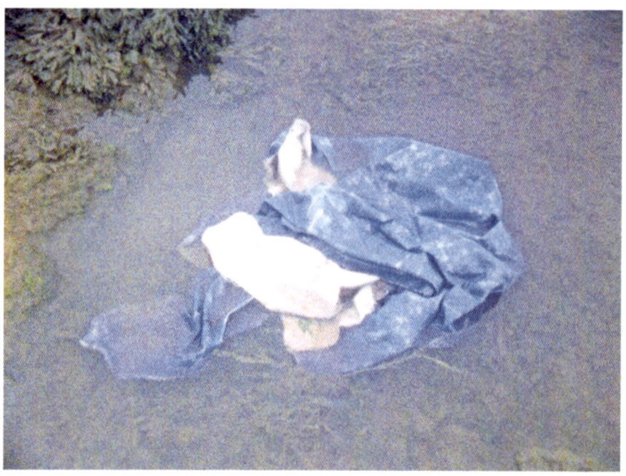
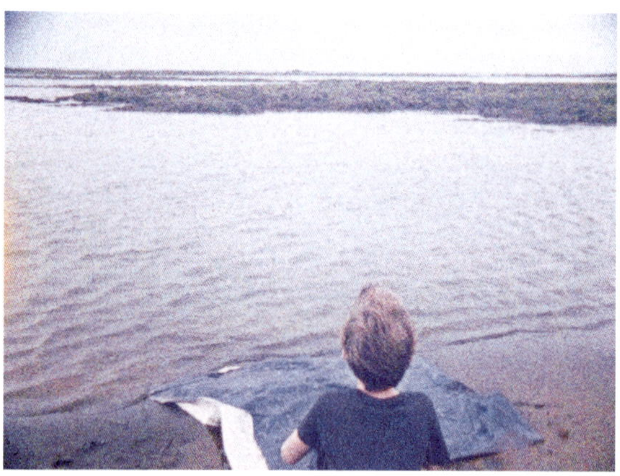

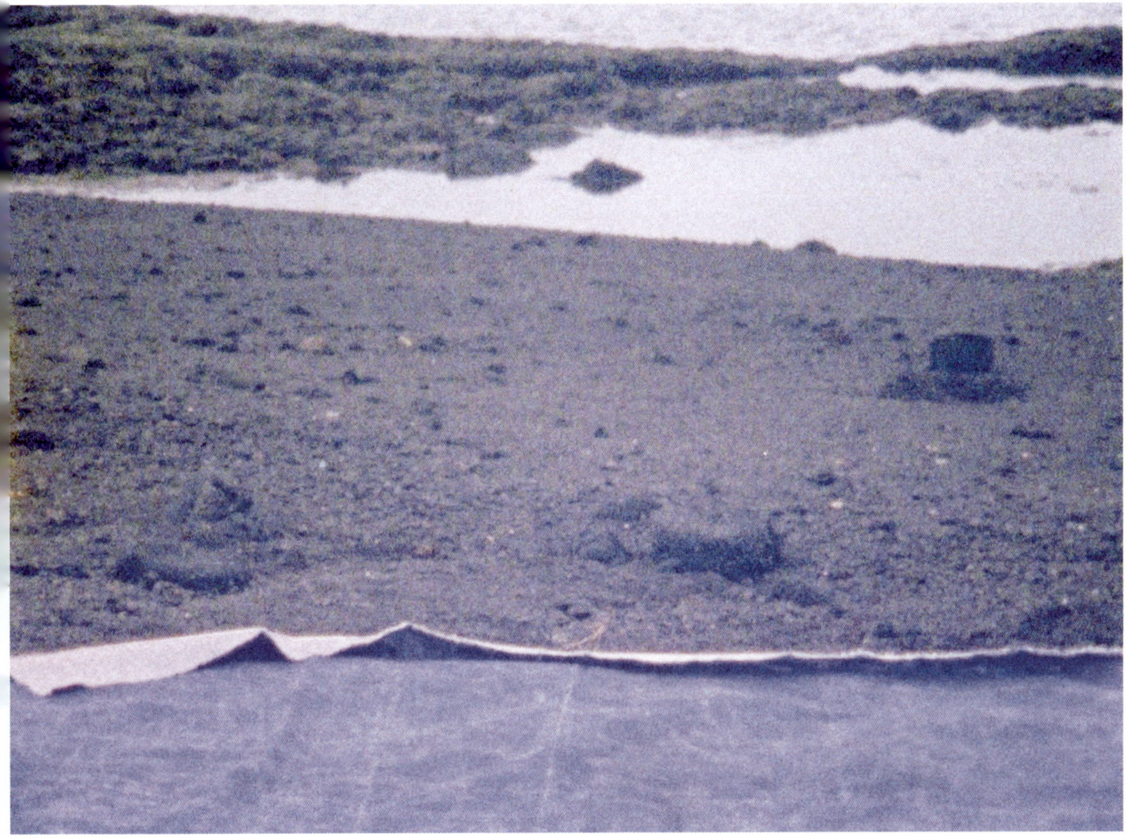

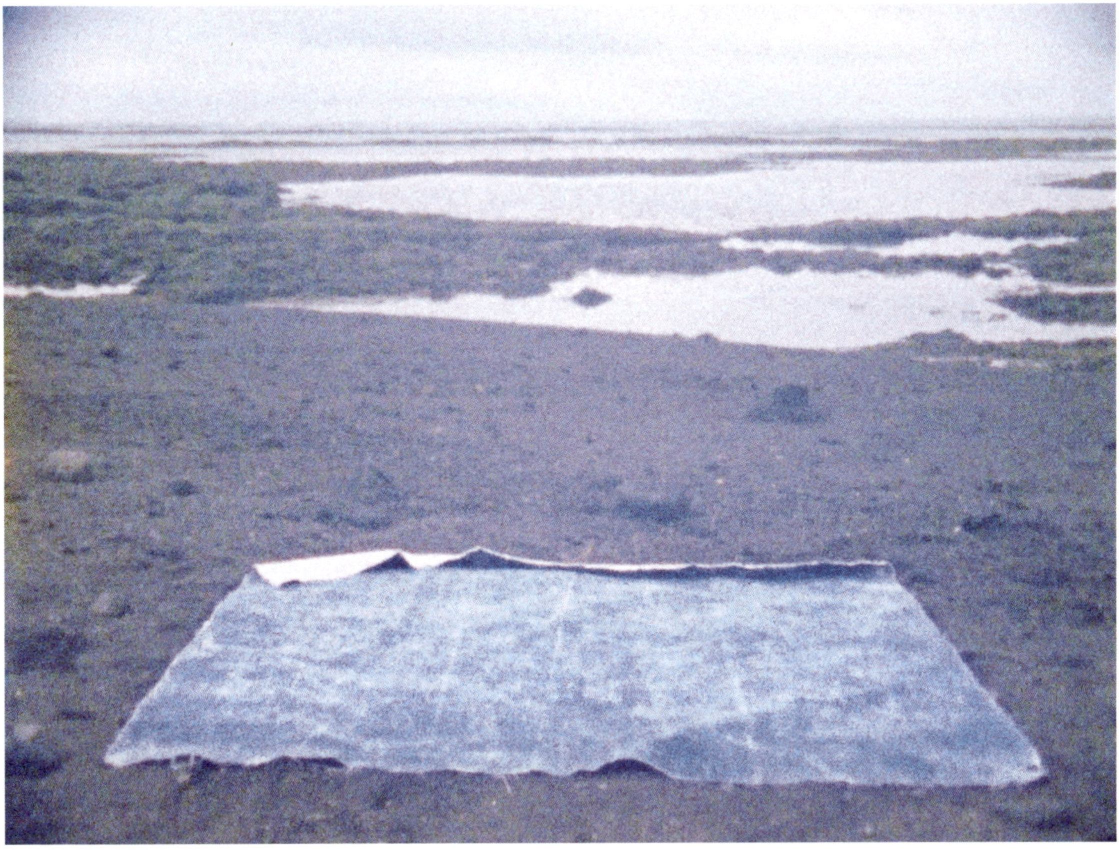

Fallende Körper – Wechselbeziehungen zwischen Film, Malerei und Skulptur im Werk von Elín Jakobsdóttir

Eva Scharrer

In the First Place, der Titel von Elín Jakobsdóttirs Ausstellung in der Schwartzschen Villa impliziert sowohl eine zeitliche wie auch eine räumliche Ebene. *In the First Place* stellt etwas an erste Stelle in einer Bedeutungshierarchie – wörtlich übersetzt bedeutet es soviel wie sich an einem primären Ort zu befinden. Die Künstlerin kehrt damit in gewisser Weise zurück zu ihren Ursprüngen – biographisch und künstlerisch – und schließt einen Zyklus.

In dem gleichnamigen Film besucht Jakobsdóttir den Ort ihrer Kindheit – das Haus ihrer Urgroßeltern in Eyrarbakki im Süden Islands. Nicht weit des Vulkans Hekla, der 1970 ausbrach als die Künstlerin gerade zwei Jahre alt war, und ihre Familie überraschend zur Flucht veranlasste. Der Erzählung nach liefen sie mit Töpfen auf den Köpfen zum Land Rover, um sich vor herabfallenden Lavabrocken zu schützen. Diese Szene, mit ihrem ungewollten Slapstick und der real drohenden Gefahr durch die bewegten, brodelnden Gesteinsmassen wurde zu einer treibenden Kraft in Jakobsdóttirs Werk. Zum ersten Mal bringt sie hier zwei parallele Stränge ihrer Arbeit – Malerei und die 2000 in Paris begonnene Beschäftigung mit Super-8 und 16-mm-Film – in einer Ausstellung zusammen.

In einigen Sequenzen des Films sieht man gerahmte Schwarzweißfotografien (etwa zwischen 1900 und 1950 aufgenommen) von Verwandten in isländischer Tracht im Inneren des Hauses, dazwischen Gebrauchsgegenstände wie eine alte Nähmaschine oder eine Balkenwaage. Der auf 8 mm geschossene Film ist jedoch weniger ein Dokument zur Familien- oder Zeitgeschichte, sondern eine Reflexion über Malerei. Die Protagonisten sind ein neunjähriger Junge und ein Stück ungespannte Leinwand, auf einer Seite Himmelblau bemalt. In den ersten Sequenzen hievt der Junge die zu einem Sack geformte Leinwand mit blauem Innenleben durch ein Fenster nach Außen und lässt sie fallen – wie einen Sandsack der als Ballast abgeworfen wird. In der nächsten Sequenz schleppt er sie im Haus eine Treppe herauf, um sie von weiter oben abzuwerfen – doch die Leinwand verschwindet nicht. Sie kehrt immer wieder zurück und geht schließlich mit auf die Reise, vom Studio der Künstlerin in Glasgow in das alte Haus nach Island. Dort wird sie über den Boden geschleift, auf Stühle gesetzt, wie eine wehende Fahne über eine Wiese gezogen und einen steinigen Weg entlanggezerrt, bis ans Ufer des Nordatlantischen Ozeans und schließlich dem Wasser übergeben.

Das Motiv des Leinwandsacks – einerseits Ballast, der vergeblich abgeworfen wird, anderseits Vehikel für Begehren und Träume – ist einem der ersten Filme von Elín Jakobsdóttir
S. 91 entnommen (*Sleeping Bag*, 2000). Ihr Fallen und das Eintauchen in das dunkle Meerwasser knüpfen an die jüngsten Gemälde der Künstlerin an, in denen nur als Umrisszeichnung wiedergegebene Körper durch liquide Farbfelder in unbekannte Tiefen
S. 43 zu stürzen scheinen. In dem Bild *Joan and the Whale* (2019) etwa sinken die Umrisse einer weiblichen Figur mit angewinkelt gespreizten Beinen und wie zum Schutz erhobenen Händen in eine aquarische Schlucht, in der sich wie in einem Schattentheater bedrohliche, an Knochen, Skelette oder Korallenriffe erinnernde Strukturen abzeichnen. Der Titel verweist auf den biblischen Propheten Jona, der auf der Flucht vor einem Befehl Gottes auf einem Schiff in einen Sturm gerät, als dessen Verursacher er von den Seeleuten über Bord geworfen wird und von einem Walfisch verschluckt wird, der ihn nach drei Tagen der Buße wieder ausspuckt. Durch ein einfaches Wortspiel wird aus Jona Joan – die patriarchale, männlich konnotierte Rolle des Propheten wird subversiv auf eine weibliche Figur übertragen, die im Innern des Wals mit sich selbst ringt.

Noch dynamischer scheint sich das Eintauchen in
S. 45 *The End of Things* (2019) zu ereignen. Eine umrisshafte Gestalt – oder sind es zwei? – ohne erkennbares Geschlecht stürzt kopfüber in ein bewegtes Purpur. Die Szene erinnert an einen barocken Höllensturz, voller Dramatik und Komik. Oben zappeln zwei Beine, während an anderer Stelle ein Paar einzelner Füße nur durch Fäden mit dem sich bereits in Auflösung und Transformation begriffenen Körper verbunden sind, aus dem sich auch schon die Eingeweide zu lösen und ein Eigenleben zu führen scheinen. Hinter den roten und

blaugrünen Umrissen der fallenden Figur erscheint ein dunkler, verzweigter Schatten vor einem rosaroten Licht.

Alle Gemälde sind geprägt von der Dualität zwischen sinnlich lasierender Malerei und Binnenkontur, Abstraktion und Figuration, amorpher Masse und indexikalischen Zeichen. Elín Jakobsdóttir arbeitet sich dabei an zwei Strängen der Moderne ab: der puren Form und der Erforschung des Unterbewussten. Zufall und Prozess, Spiel und Experiment sind sowohl an der Entstehung des liquiden Bildhintergrunds wie auch der Figurenzeichnung maßgeblich beteiligt: Zunächst wird stark verdünnte Acrylfarbe auf die flach auf dem Boden liegende, mit Gesso grundierte Leinwand geschüttet, deren Verläufe durch Bewegung des Malgrunds leicht manipuliert werden bis die Farbe trocknet. Dieser Vorgang wiederholt sich mehrere Male, bis dichte Farbräume entstehen deren gewachsene Strukturen entfernt an Abklatsch-, Frottage- oder Rorschach-Techniken erinnern – surreale Landschaften einer inneren Welt voller psychologisch aufgeladener Tropen. Die Figuren wiederum entwickeln sich aus schnellen, automatischen Zeichnungen in surrealistischer Tradition, deren Bewegungen sich als unterbewusst erinnerte Körpersprache in das physische Gedächtnis einprägen und dann in Öl auf Leinwand übertragen werden. Daraus entsteht ein Code aus wiederkehrenden Formen und Symbolen.

Das Motiv gespreizter oder auch abgetrennter Beine taucht mehrfach auf – etwa in dem Gemälde *Hollow Legs* S. 51
(2021). Hier erscheint der fragmentierte, konstruierte Körper in verschiedenen Zuständen zwischen Gebären und Sezession vor einem blutroten Hintergrund. In *Insomniac* (2018) berührt S. 49
eine in Rot sitzende geschlechtslose Figur mit einer Hand eine rechteckige Form, die ein Tafelbild oder auch ein Fenster darstellen könnte. Dieselbe Geste taucht wiederum im Film auf, wenn der Junge die Scheibe des Fensters berührt, durch das er später den Leinwandsack werfen wird. In einer späteren Filmsequenz zeichnet er die blaue Silhouette einer Figur auf die Scheibe, in der er sich gleichzeitig selbst spiegelt. Wieder später malt er eine blaue Figur auf eine Leinwand, bevor er diese schließlich ganz mit blauer Farbe ausfüllt. Der Film loopt.

Das permanente Wechselspiel von Innen und Außen – beziehungsweise die Gleichzeitigkeit beider Zustände – ist ein zentrales Motiv in Elín Jakobsdóttirs Gemälden und Zeichnungen, im Film sowie in den skulpturalen Arbeiten. Die Figuren zeigen stets ihr Innenleben – innere Organe wie Magen, Nieren, Lunge, Uterus, Gehirn – sowie ihre diversen Körperöffnungen und äußeren Sinnesorgane. Gleichzeitig fließt die Außenwelt als Farbe durch sie hindurch.

Diese Transparenz ist auch Gegenstand der Papierschneidearbeiten (Paper Cut-outs), deren Strukturen an dichtes Blattwerk, Gefieder oder Gewebe erinnern. In der Skulptur S. 92 *Two Sided Table* (2008) sind sie gefasst in einer hölzernen Konstruktion auf vier Beinen, zwischen Glasplatten die sowohl horizontal als auch vertikal ausgerichtet sind, so dass sich das schwarze Gespinst in unterschiedliche Richtungen entfalten kann.

Als Hybrid aus Tisch und Fenster evoziert die Skulptur eine Situation, in der sich zwei Menschen gegenübersitzen und anblicken, aber durch eine Glasscheibe voneinander getrennt sind. Die Form der Konstruktion erinnert auch an perspektivische Zeichenhilfen, wie sie etwa Albrecht Dürer in seiner Buchillustration *Der Zeichner des liegenden Weibes* (zwischen 1512 und 1525) darstellte. Es ist eine absurde Sehmaschine, die den Blick gleichzeitig verschleiert, fragmentiert und optisch animiert.

Die Struktur des Cut-out selbst erzeugt eine Art Op-Art-Effekt, als blicke man auf eine lebendige, dreidimensionale Masse, die sich bewegt und Beulen ausbildet. Man könnte darin auch die Eruption und die poröse schwarze Kruste fließender Lava erkennen, vor der Jakobsdóttirs Familie einst floh. Zwischen den Glasplatten ist die Gefahr gebannt, die Schönheit der Materie lässt sich betrachten wie unter dem Mikroskop. Die physische Bewegung, die ein Bild entstehen lässt, die kontrollierte Turbulenz und die Transparenz des Körpers verweist wieder zurück auf die Gemälde. Wenn auch mit ganz anderen Mitteln erforscht Elín Jakobsdóttir in den verschiedenen Medien – Film, Malerei und Cut-Out/Skulptur – Wege der physischen und mentalen Erfahrbarkeit in einer steten, elliptischen Bewegung zwischen innerer und äußerer Welt.

Falling Bodies – Interrelations between Film, Painting and Sculpture in the Work of Elín Jakobsdóttir

Eva Scharrer

In the First Place, the title of Elín Jakobsdóttir's exhibition at the Schwartzsche Villa, implies a temporal as well as a spatial level of meaning. The phrase 'in the first place' puts something in the prime position of a hierarchy of significance – taken literally, it would mean finding ourselves in the original place. Thus, in a certain sense, the artist is going back to her (biographical and artistic) origins and completing a cycle.

In her film of the same name, Jakobsdóttir visits a site important in her childhood: her great-grandparents' house in Eyrarbakki, on the south coast of Iceland. It is not far from the volcano Hekla, whose eruption in 1970 led to the sudden evacuation of the two-year-old artist and her family. As the story goes, they ran to their Land Rover with cooking pots on their heads to protect them from falling chunks of lava. With its unintentional slapstick and the genuinely threatening menace of the moving and seething masses of rock, this scene has become a driving force in Jakobsdóttir's work. Now, for the first time, she is bringing together in a single exhibition two parallel strands of her work: her painting and her occupation with Super8 and 16mm film, which began in Paris in 2000.

Several sequences from the film feature framed black-and-white photographs (taken between 1900 and 1950) of relatives seen in traditional Icelandic dress inside the house's interior; between them, we see devices like an old sewing machine or a set of scales. However, this film shot on 8mm stock is less a documentation of family or social history than a reflection on painting. Its protagonists are a nine-year-old boy and a piece of unstretched canvas that has been painted sky blue on one side. The opening sequences show the canvas, formed into the shape of a bag with a blue interior, being hauled through a window by the boy and allowed to fall – like a sandbag cast off as ballast. In the next sequence, he hauls it up a stairway inside the house in order to throw it out from further up, but the canvas does not disappear. It comes back again and again and finally goes along on the journey from the artist's studio in Glasgow to the old house in Iceland. There it is dragged across the floor, placed on chairs, pulled across a meadow like a waving flag and yanked along a stony path all the way to the shore of the North Atlantic, where it is finally consigned to the water.

The motif of the canvas bag – which, on the one hand, is ballast cast off in vain and, on the other, a vehicle for desires and dreams – is borrowed from one of Jakobsdóttir's first p. 91 films *Sleeping Bag*, (2000). Its falling and its immersion in the dark waters of the sea are linked to the artist's most recent paintings, in which bodies represented solely in the form of outline drawings seem to plunge through liquid fields of colour and into unfathomed depths. In the painting *Joan and* p. 43 *the Whale* (2019), for example, the outlines of a female figure – with legs spread and bent at the knees and hands raised as if to protect herself – sink into an aquatic ravine, where menacing formations reminiscent of bones, skeletons or coral reefs stand out in a manner that recalls a shadow theatre. The title alludes to the Biblical prophet Jonah who, attempting to flee God's command by boarding a ship, finds himself in a storm: as the cause of the storm, he is thrown overboard by the sailors and swallowed by a whale, which spits him out again after three days of penance. Through a simple play on words, Jonah becomes Joan, subversively transferring the patriarchal and stereotypically masculine role of the prophet to a female figure who comes to grips with herself inside the whale.

This immersion seems to take place in an even more p. 45 dynamic manner in *The End of Things* (2019). A silhouette-like figure – or is it two? – of unidentifiable gender plunges head first into a fluid purple. The scene recalls a Baroque Fall of the Damned, full of dramatic and comic elements. Two legs flail around at the top while nothing but strings connect a pair of individual feet to the body, which is already in the midst of a process of disintegration and transformation and whose entrails also already seem to be removing themselves from inside it and leading a life of their own. Behind the falling figure's red and blue-green contours, a dark branching shadow appears in front of a pink light.

All paintings are shaped by the dualism between the use of sensually applied washes and interior contours, abstraction and figuration, amorphous mass and indexical sign. Within this context, Jakobsdóttir has devoted herself to pursuing two strands of modern art: pure form and the exploration of the subconscious. Chance and process, play and experimentation perform a decisive role in the creation of her paintings' fluid backgrounds as well as their figure drawing. Highly diluted acrylic paint is first poured out onto the canvas, which is primed with gesso and laid out flat on the ground. The course of the flowing colours is manipulated slightly by moving the canvas until the paint has dried. This process is repeated multiple times until dense chromatic spaces – whose organically developed formations vaguely recall those of transfer, frottage or Rorschach techniques – emerge as the surreal landscapes of an inner world full of psychologically charged tropes. The figures, on the other hand, develop out of rapid, automatic drawings in the Surrealist tradition, whose movements implant themselves within the physical memory as subconsciously recalled body language and are then transposed to canvas in oils. The result is a code made up of recurring forms and symbols.

The motif of spread or also detached legs appears multiple times, for example, in the painting *Hollow Legs* (2021). p. 51 Here, before a blood-red background, the fragmented and constructed bodies appear in various states between giving birth and secession. In *Insomniac* (2018) one of the hands p. 49 of the seated, sexless figure in red touches a rectangular form that could depict an easel painting or also a window. The same gesture appears once again in the film, when the boy touches the windowpane through which he will later throw the canvas bag. In a later sequence, he draws the blue silhouette of a figure on the pane in which he simultaneously casts his own reflection. Later still, he paints a blue figure on a canvas before finally filling it in completely with blue paint. The film is shown in a continuous loop.

The constant interplay of inside and out or, alternatively, the simultaneity of both states, is a central motif in Jakobsdóttir's paintings and drawings as well as her films and sculptural works. The figures always present their inner life –

internal organs like the stomach, kidneys, lungs, uterus and brain – as well as their various orifices and external sense organs. At the same time, the outside world flows through them in the form of colour.

This transparency is also the subject of her paper cut-outs, whose structures are reminiscent of dense foliage, plumage
p. 92
or textiles. In the sculpture *Two Sided Table* (2008) , the cut-outs are mounted inside a wooden construction on four legs, where they have been placed between horizontal as well as vertical sheets of glass in such a way that the black weaving can expand in different directions.

As a hybrid of a table and a window, the sculpture evokes a situation in which two people sit opposite one another and look at each other, but are separated by a sheet of glass. The construction's form is also reminiscent of perspectival drawing aids like the one depicted by Albrecht Dürer in his book illustration *Draughtsman Drawing a Reclining Nude* (between 1512 and 1525). It is an absurd seeing machine that simultaneously veils, fragments and optically animates the gaze.

The structure of the cut-out itself generates an Op Art effect, as if we were looking at a living, three-dimensional mass that was moving and bulging. This could also be identified with the eruption and porous black crust of the flowing lava that Jakobsdóttir's family once fled. The danger is held captive between the glass plates; the beauty of the material can be viewed as if it were under a microscope. The physical movement that causes an image to emerge, the controlled turbulence and the transparency of the body point back once more to the paintings. Despite her use of entirely different means, Elín Jakobsdóttir consistently explores paths of potential physical and mental experience in an elliptical movement between the inner and outer world in her various media: film, painting and cut-out/sculpture.

Joan and the Whale
Öl und Acryl auf Leinen
oil and acrylic on linen
200 × 180 cm
2020

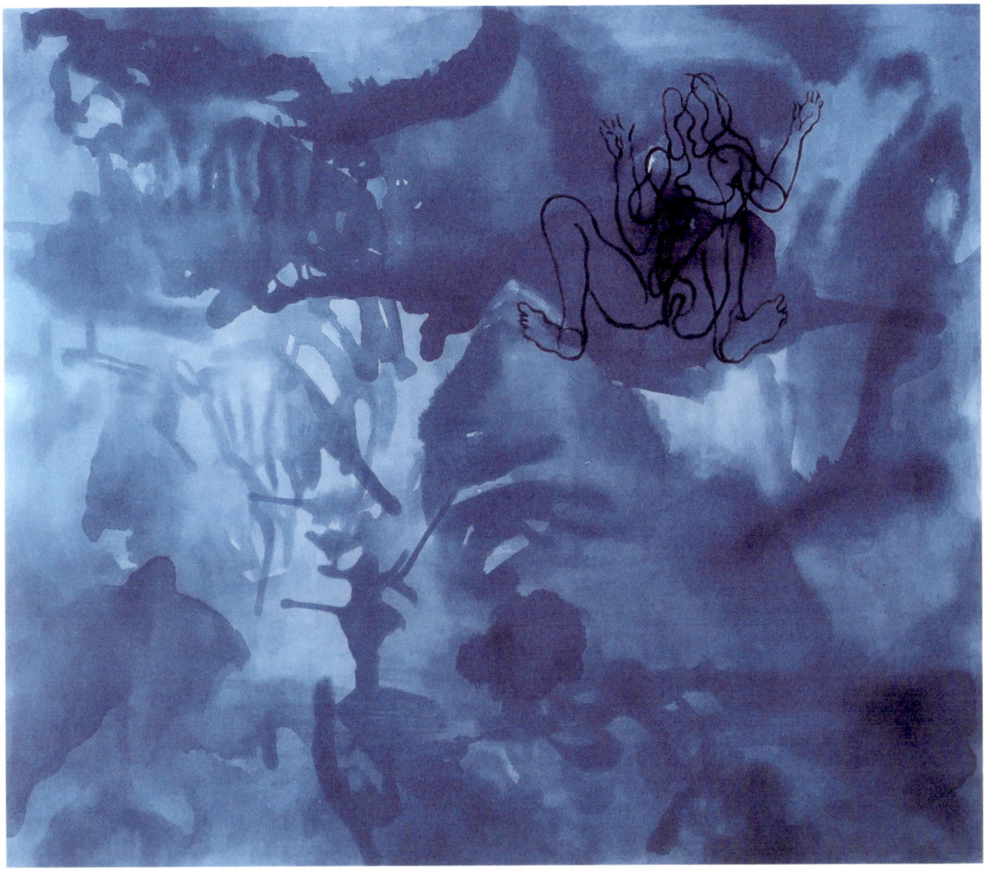

The End of Things
Öl und Acryl auf Leinen
oil and acrylic on linen
200 × 180 cm
2019

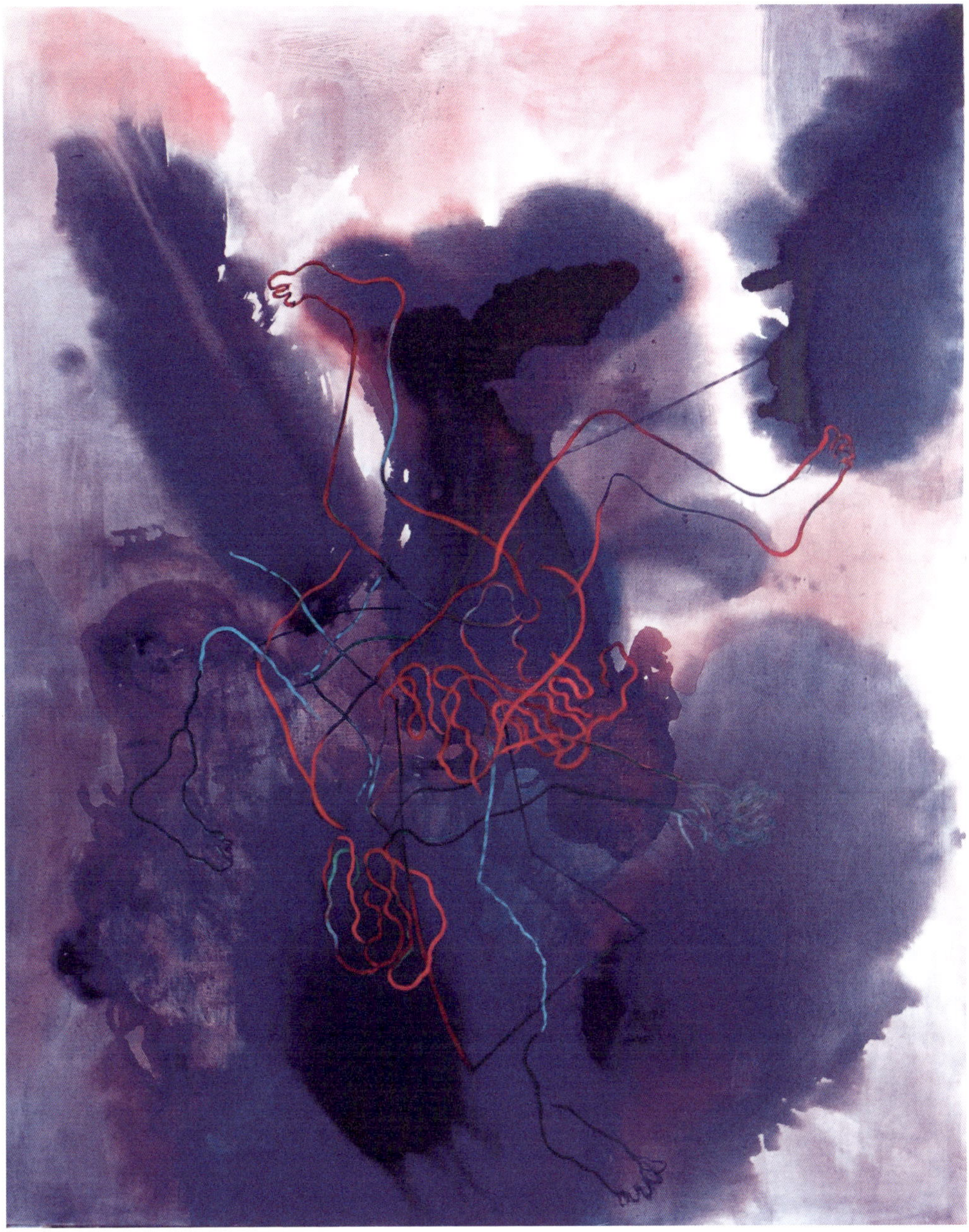

Eternal Unrest
Öl und Acryl auf Leinen
oil and acrylic on linen
2020 × 180 cm
2021

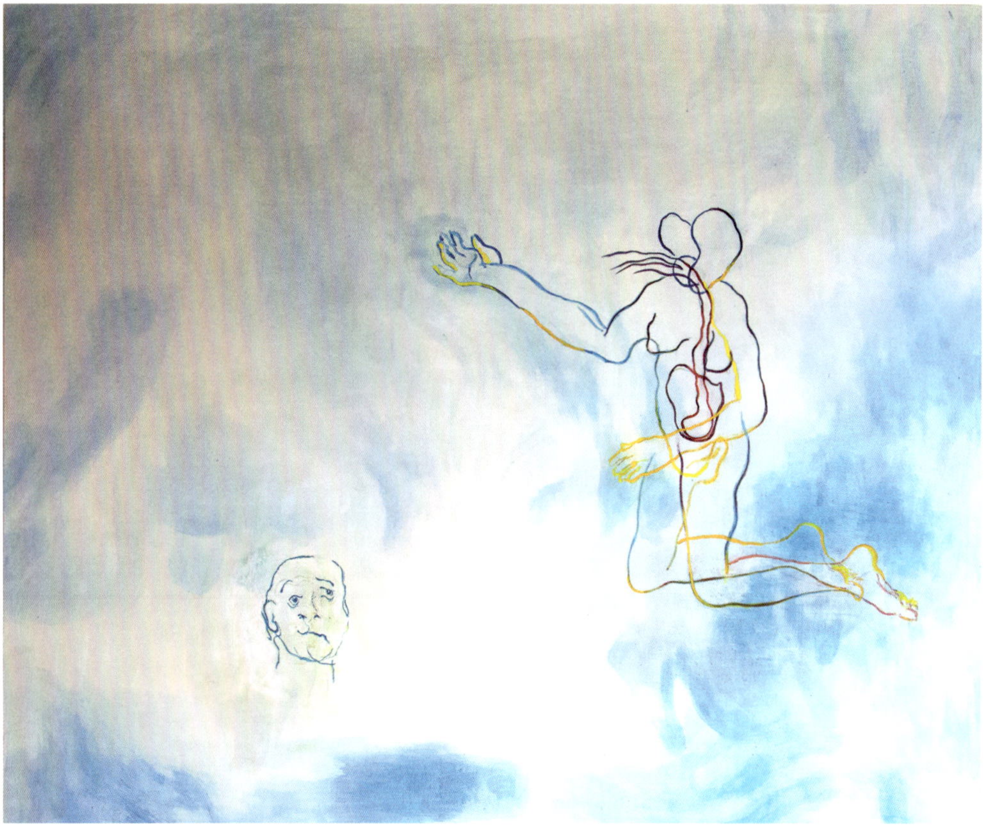

Insomniac
Öl auf Leinen
oil on linen
180 × 220 cm
2019

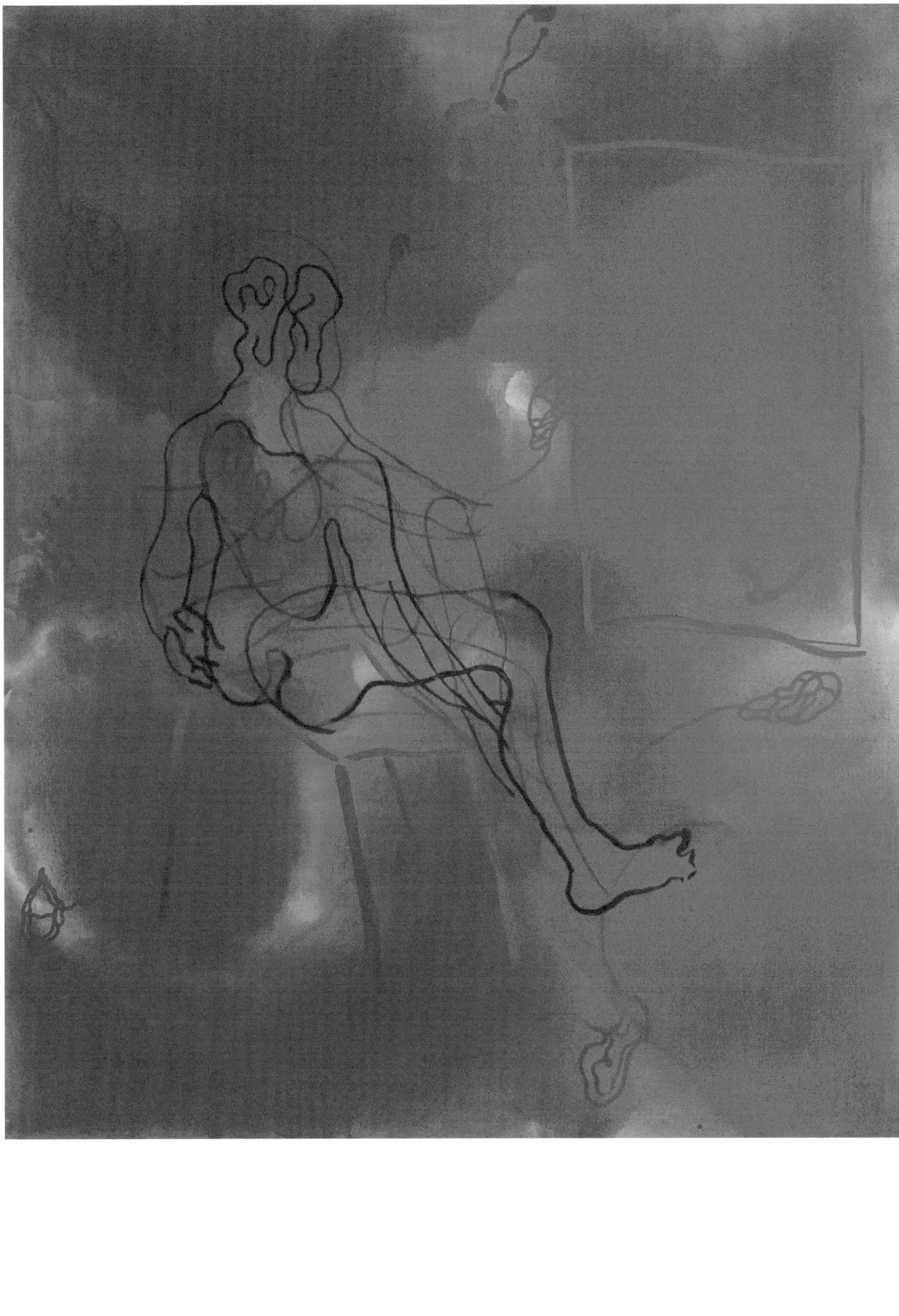

Hollow Legs
Öl und Acryl auf Leinen
oil and acrylic on linen
220 × 180 cm
2021

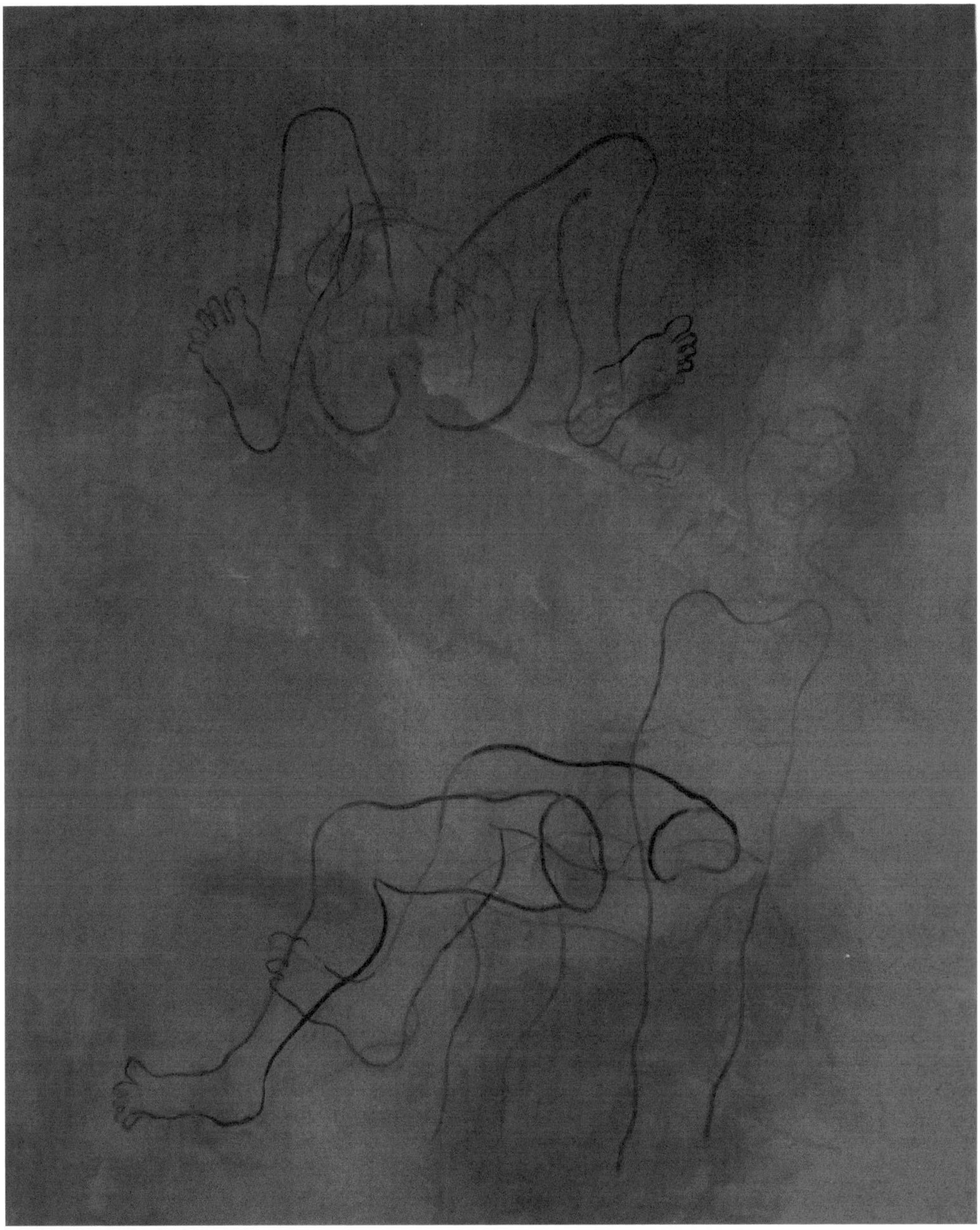

Study for Joan and the Whale
Öl auf Leinen
oil on linen
114 × 102 cm
2019

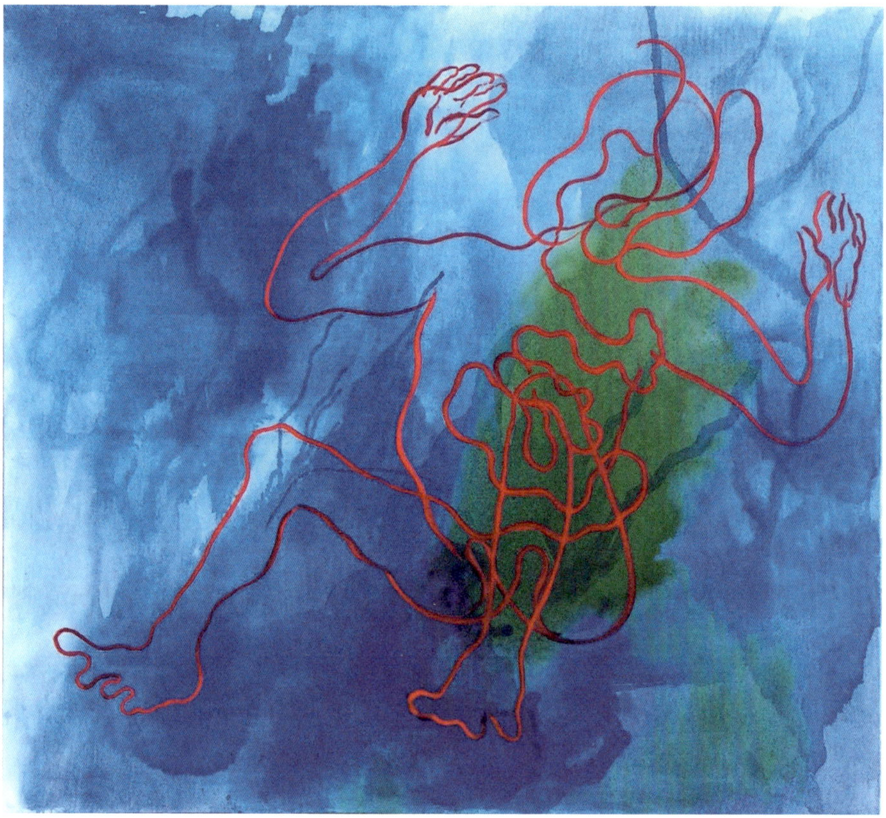

Study for Insomniac
Öl auf Leinen
oil on linen
97 × 130 cm
2019

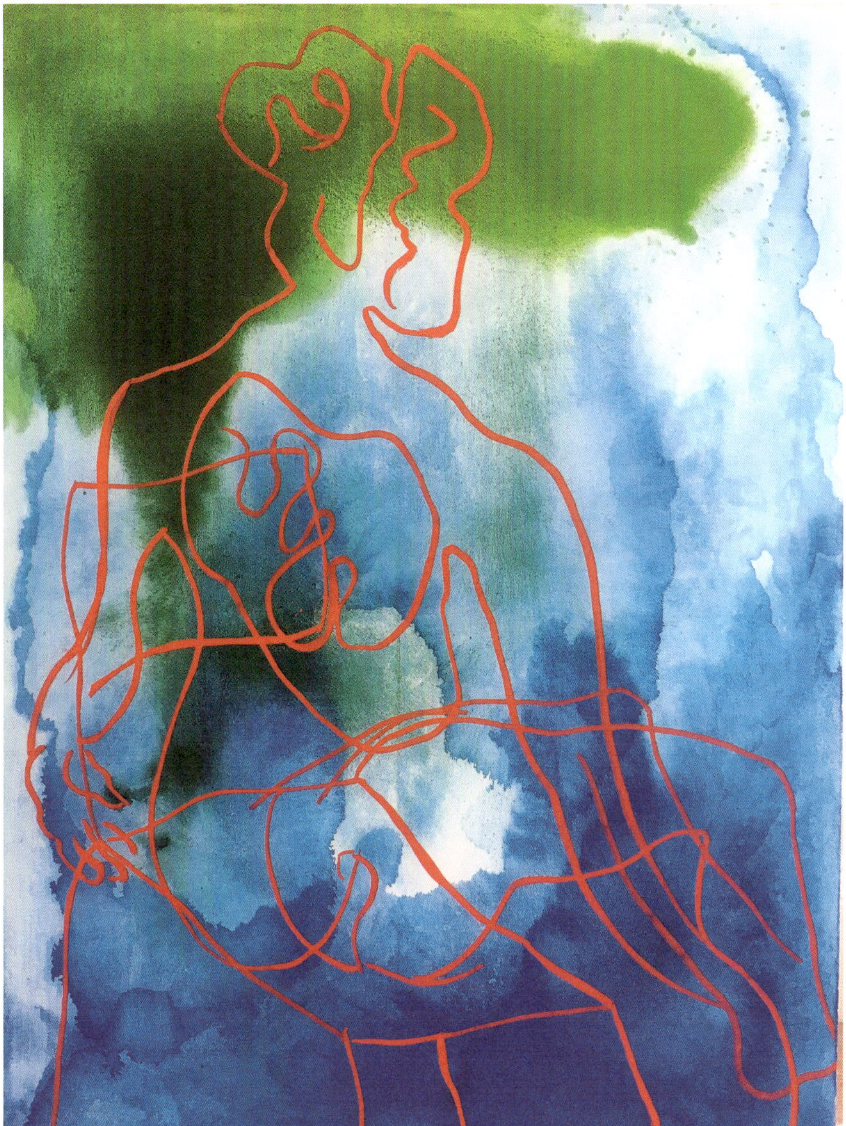

Study for Eternal Unrest
Öl auf Leinen
oil on linen
33 × 41 cm
2019

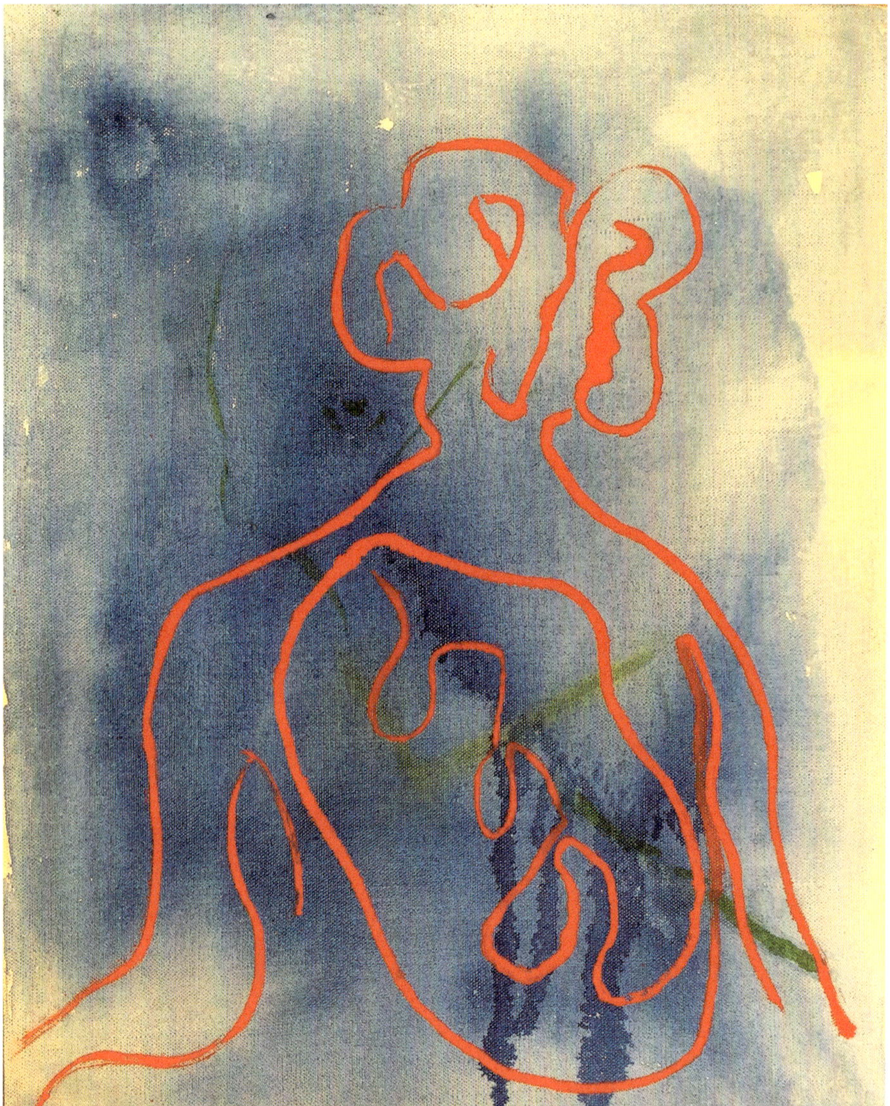

The First Big Idea
Öl auf Leinen
oil on linen
30 × 25 cm
2019

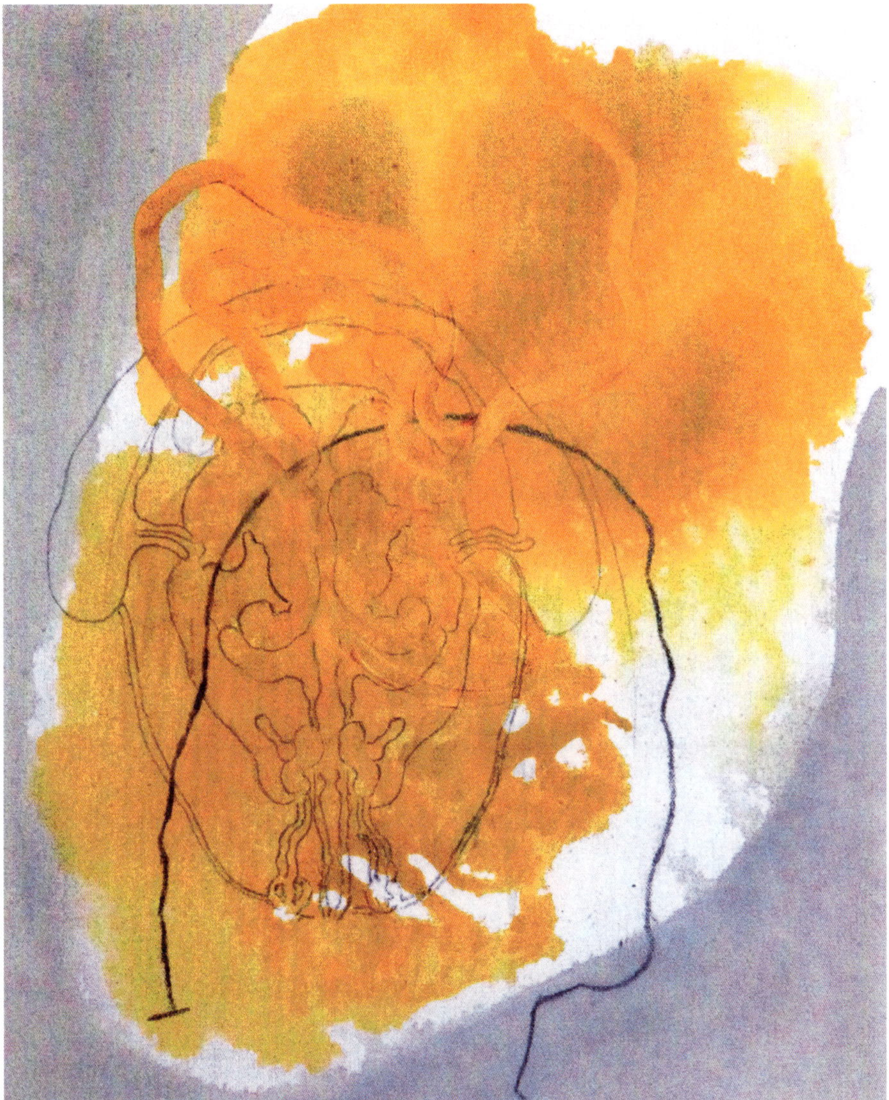

Looping Lexicon Series
Bleistift, Tinte, Gouache, Pastell, Cut-Out auf Papier
pencil, ink, gouache, pastel, cut-out, on paper
dimensions from 35 × 39 cm to 60 × 70 cm
2015–2017

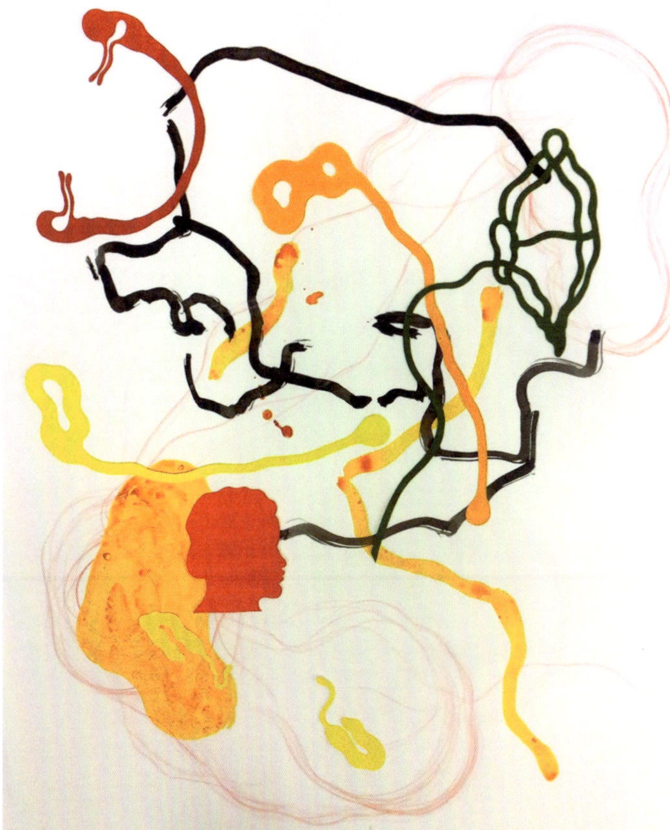

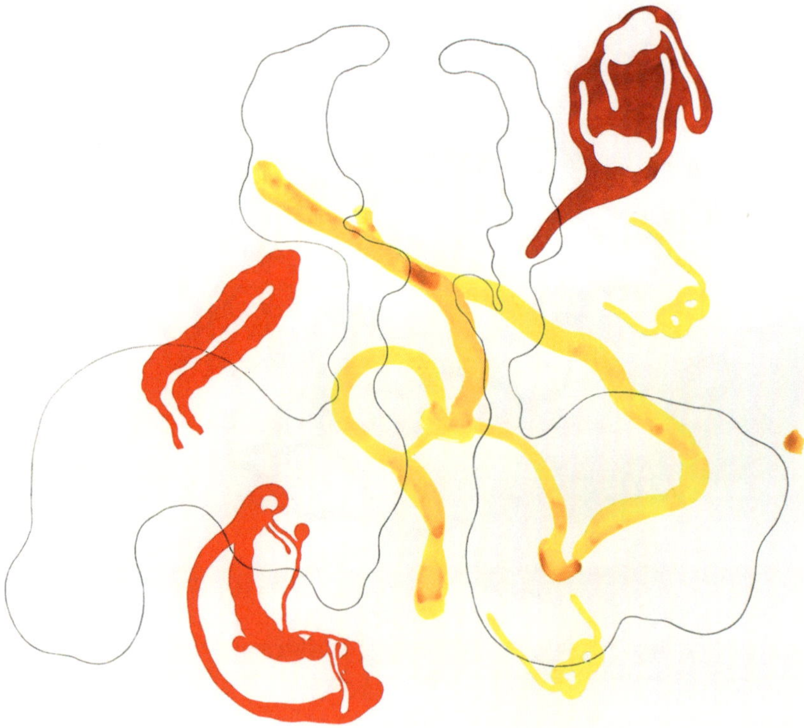

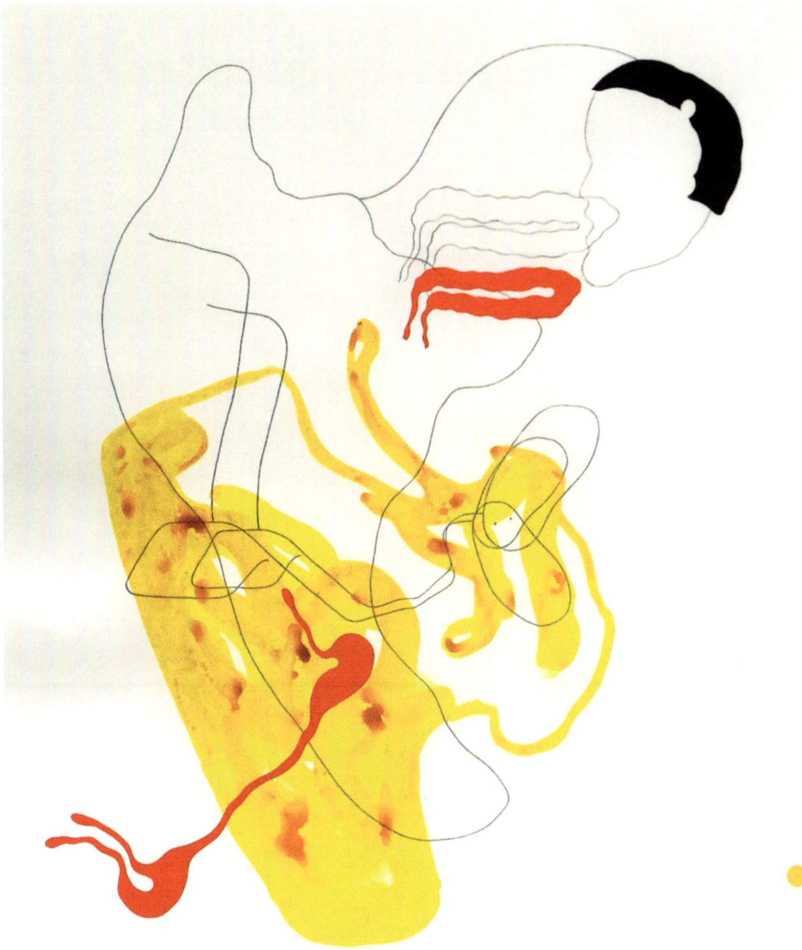

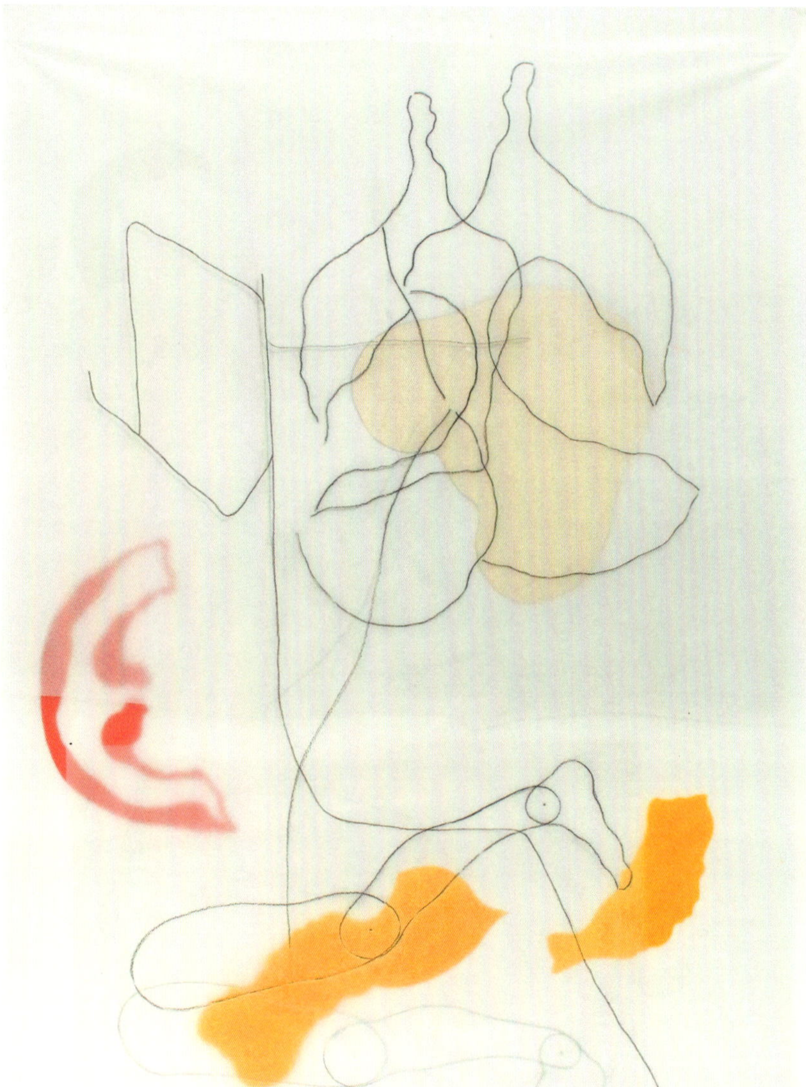

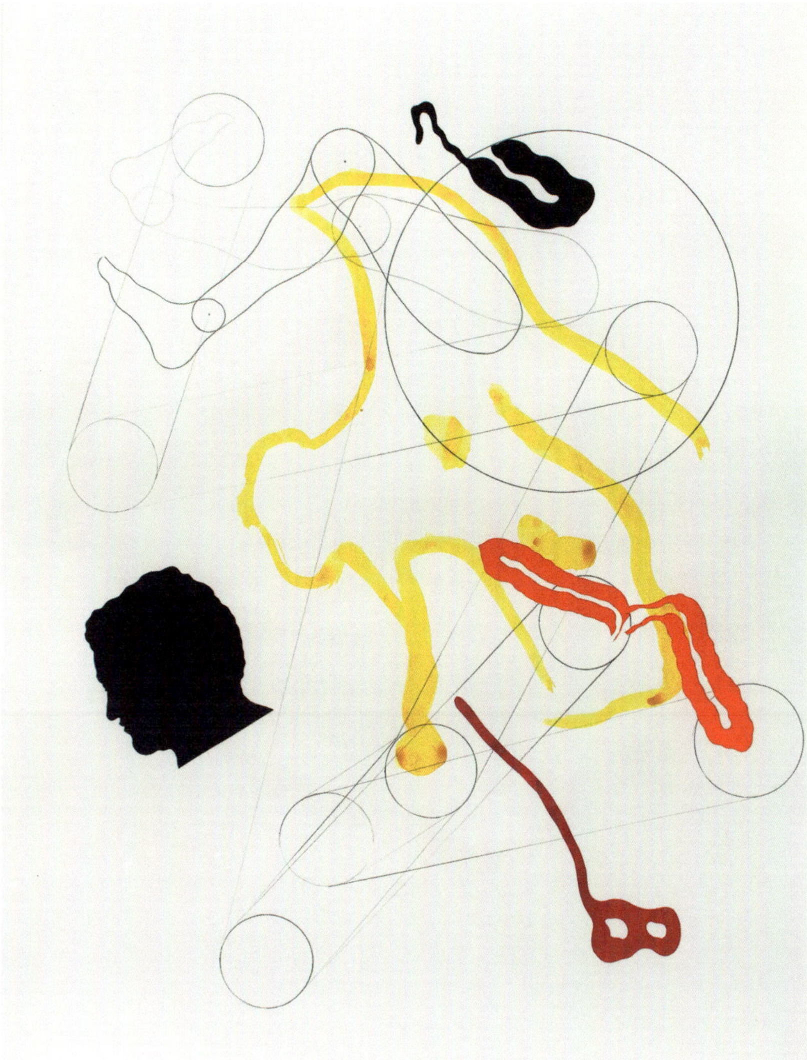

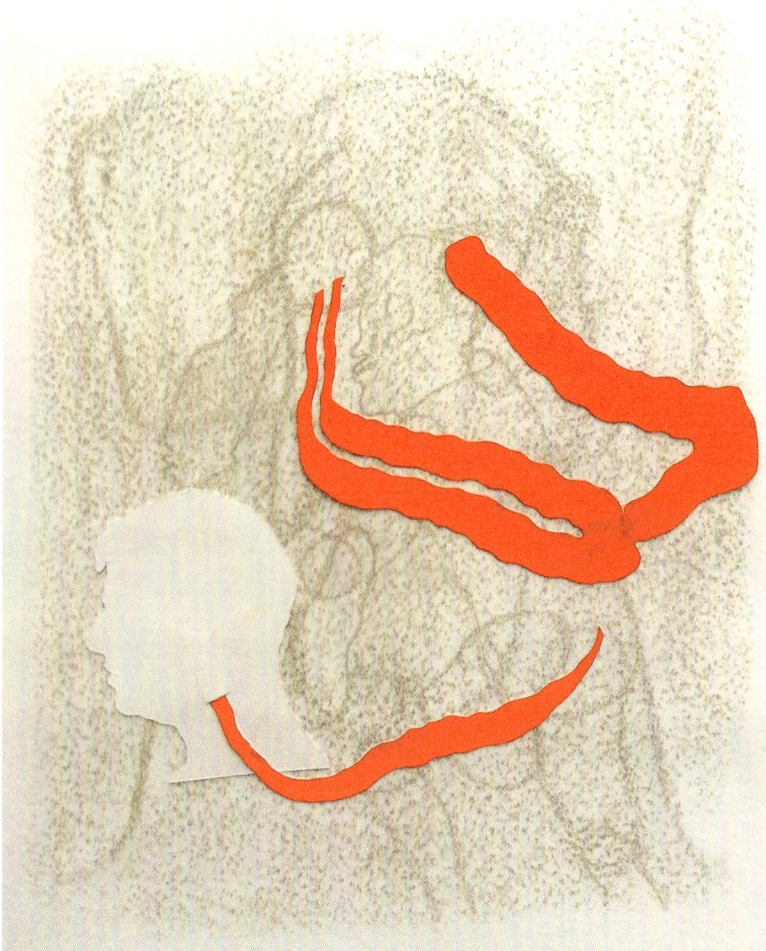

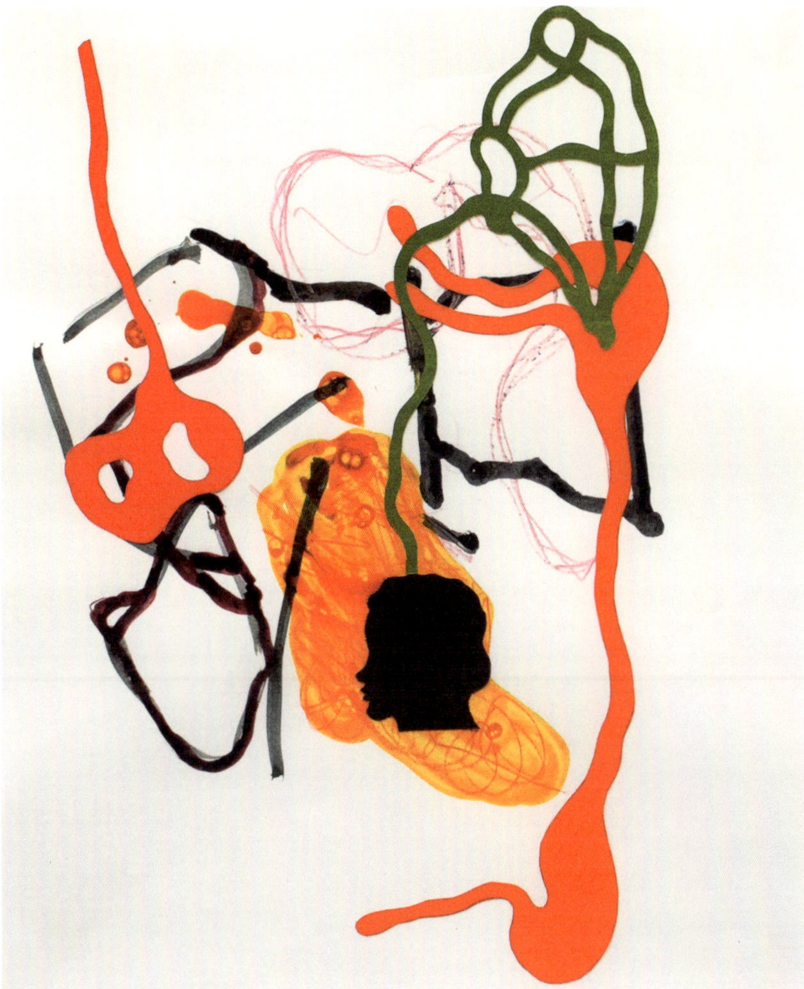

65–69, 74 Bleistift auf Papier
pencil on paper
20 × 30 cm
2019

70–71 Tinte, Bleistift auf Transparentpapier, Papier
ink, pencil, tracing paper, paper
24 × 32 cm
2020

72–73 Tinte auf Karton
ink on cardboard
24 × 33 cm
2021

75 Acryl, Perspex, Ölfarbe auf Leinwand
acrylic, perspex, oil, canvas
80 × 100 cm
2021

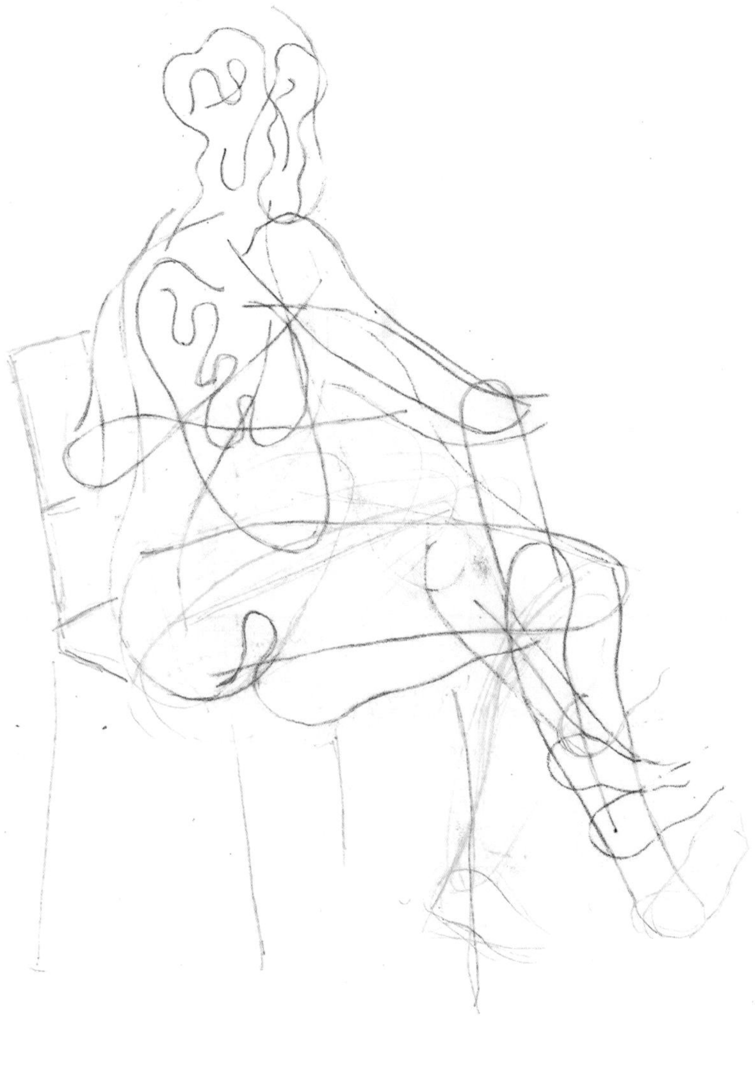

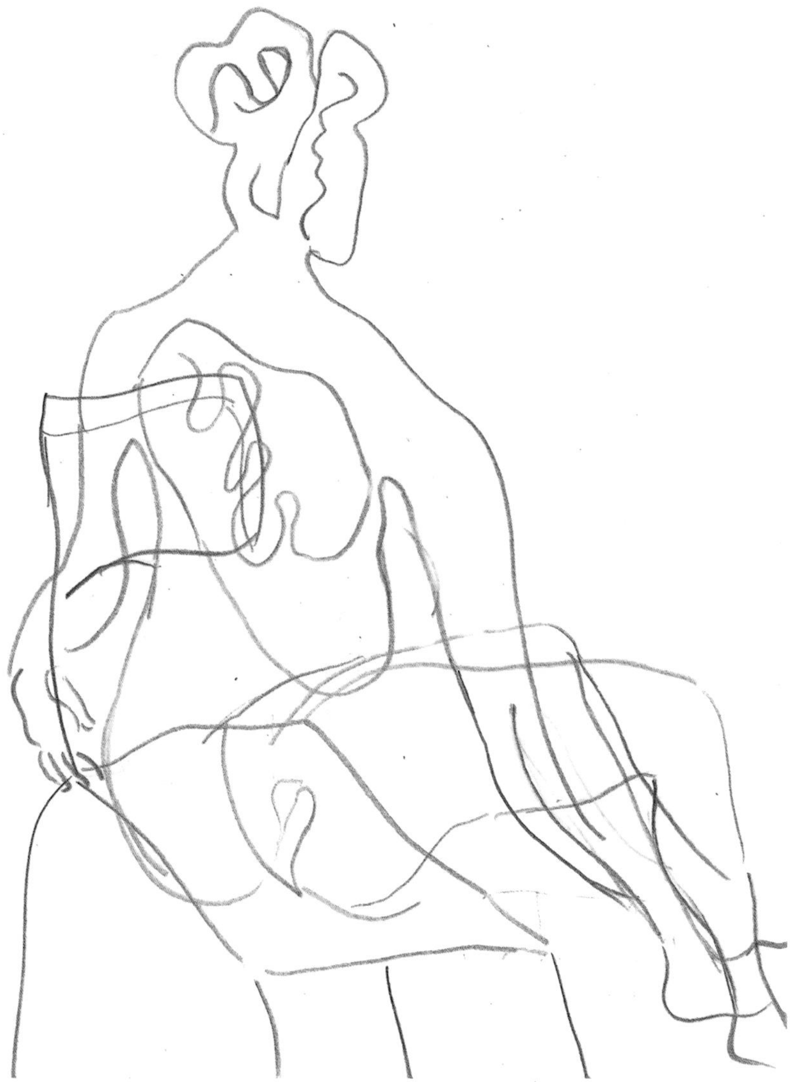

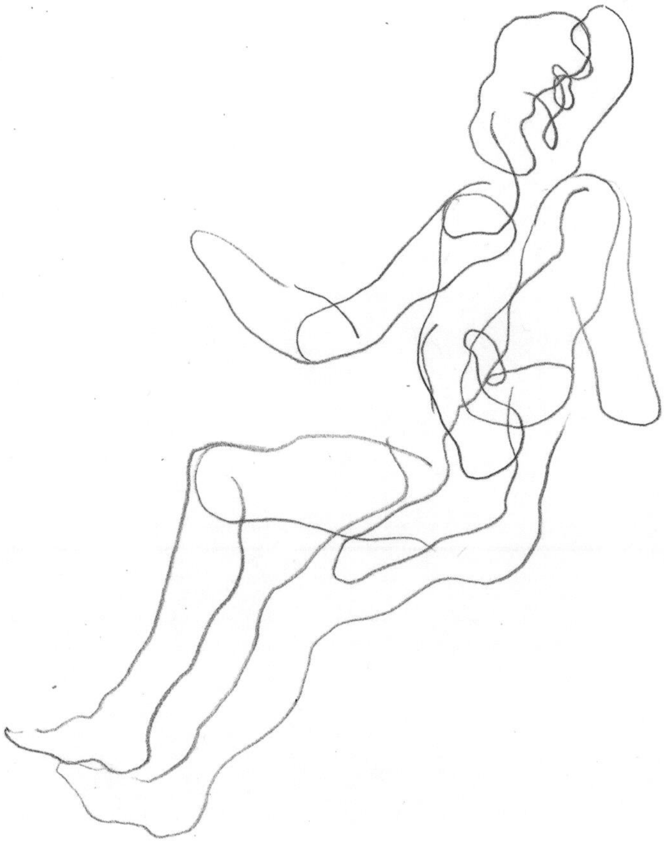

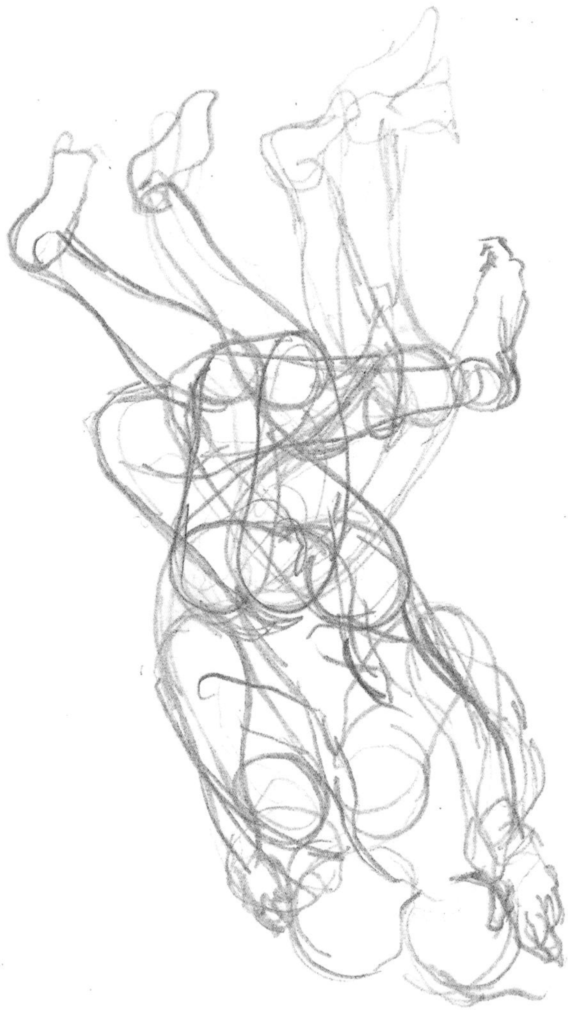

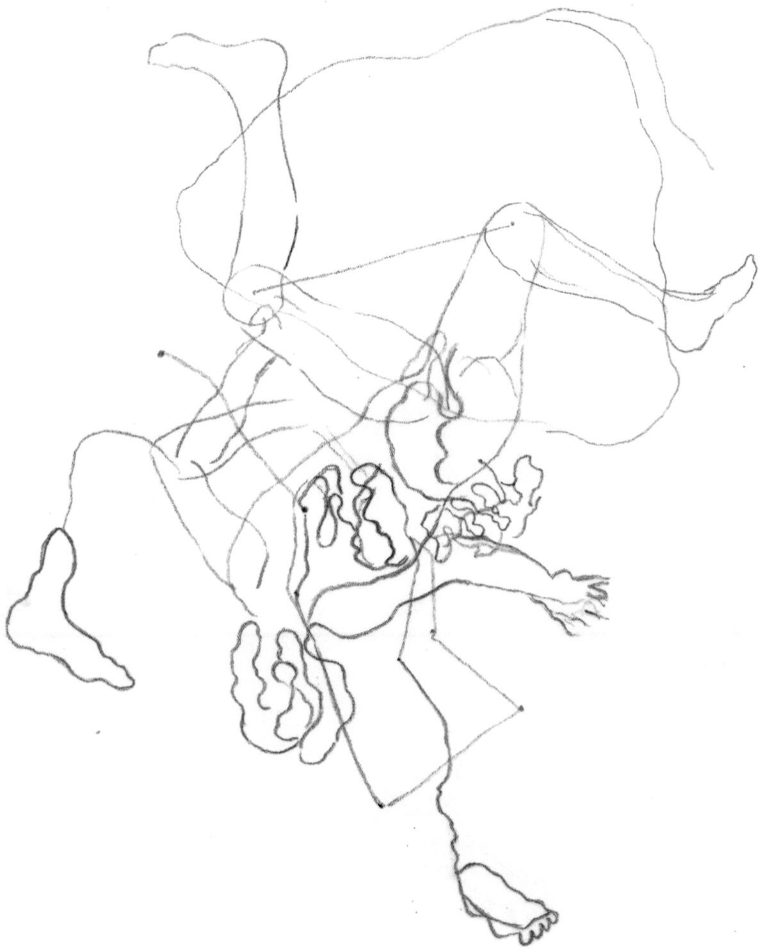

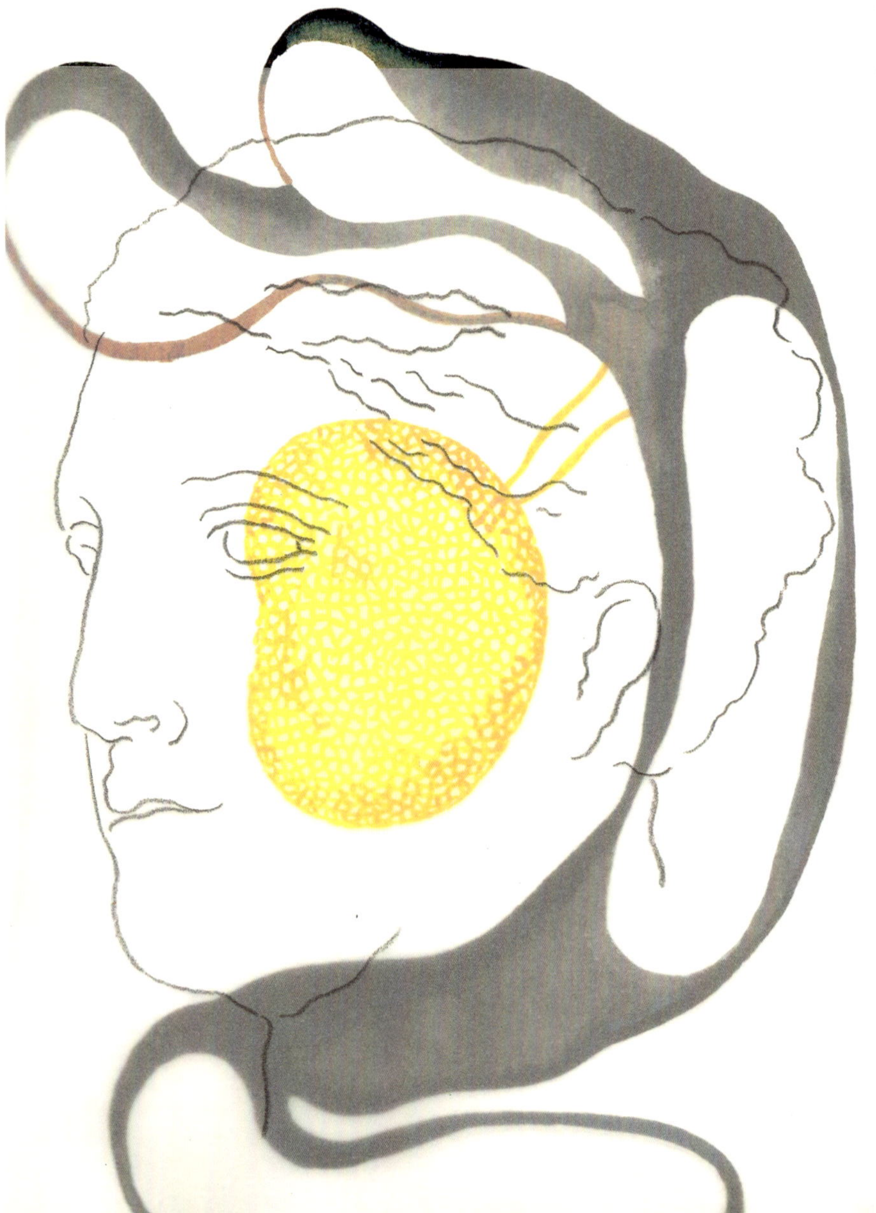

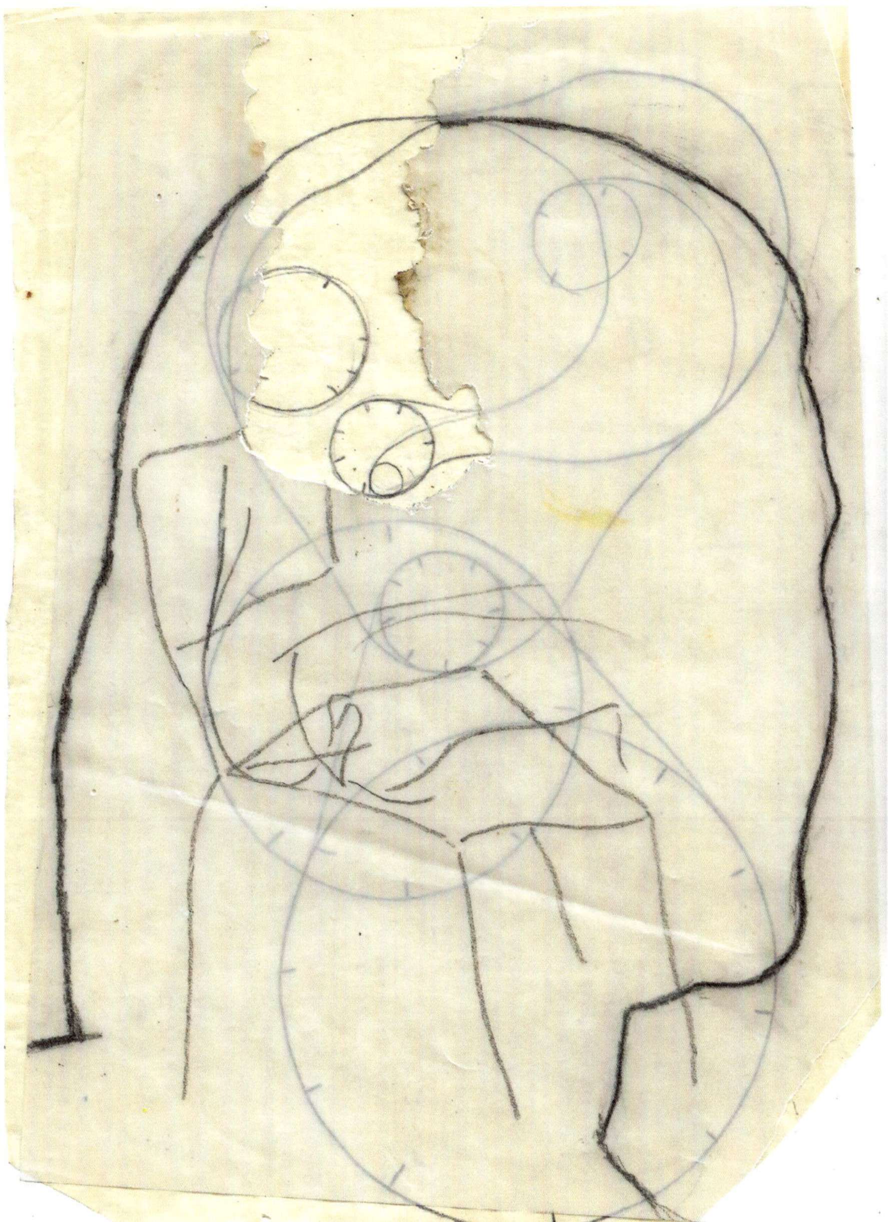

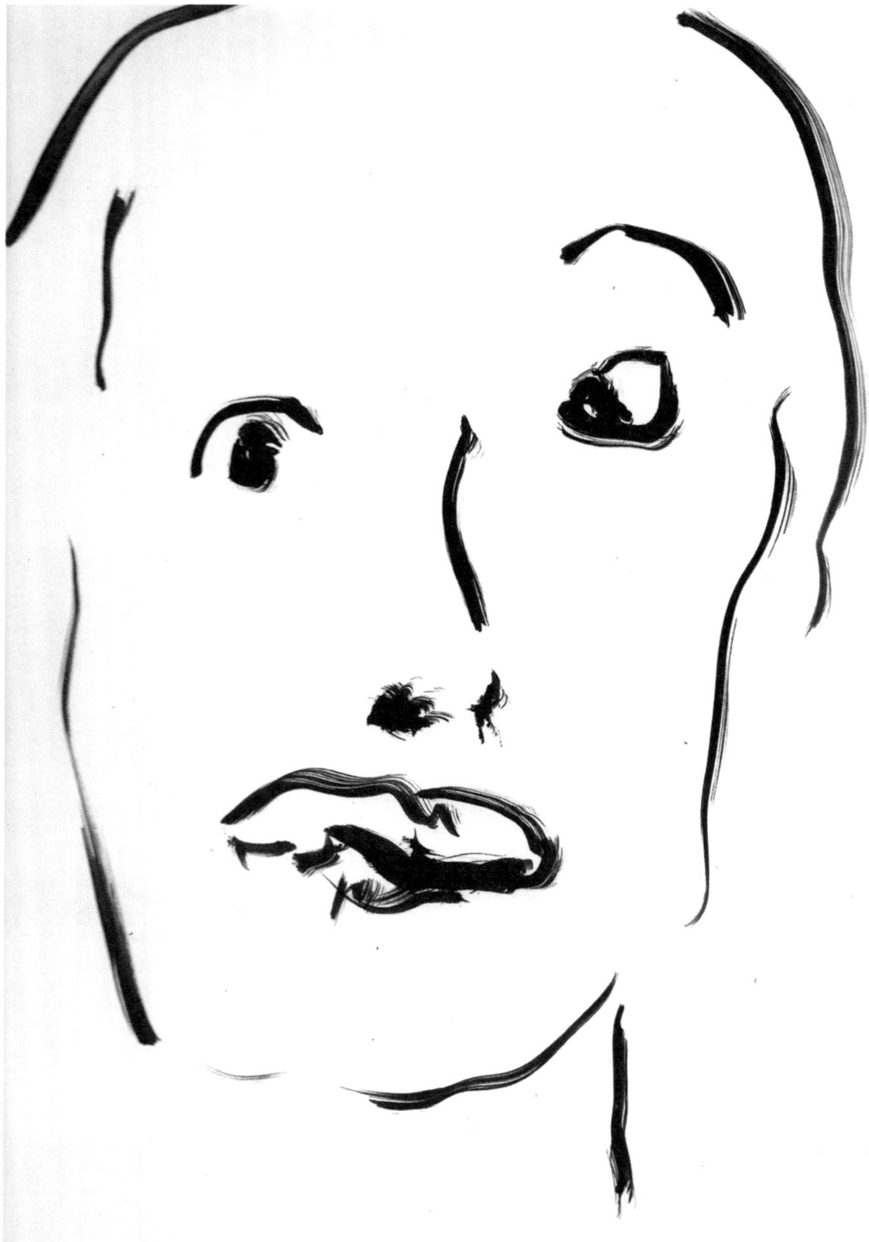

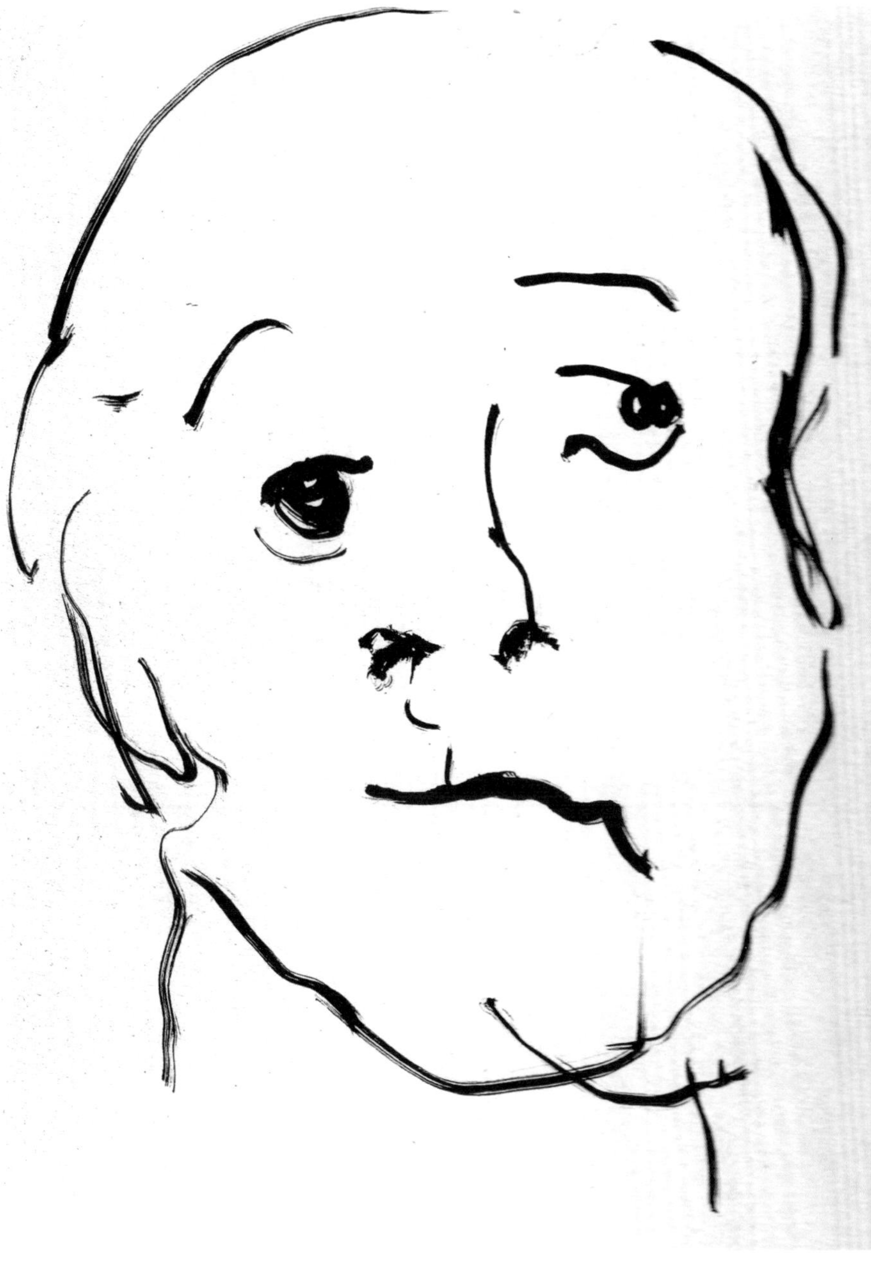

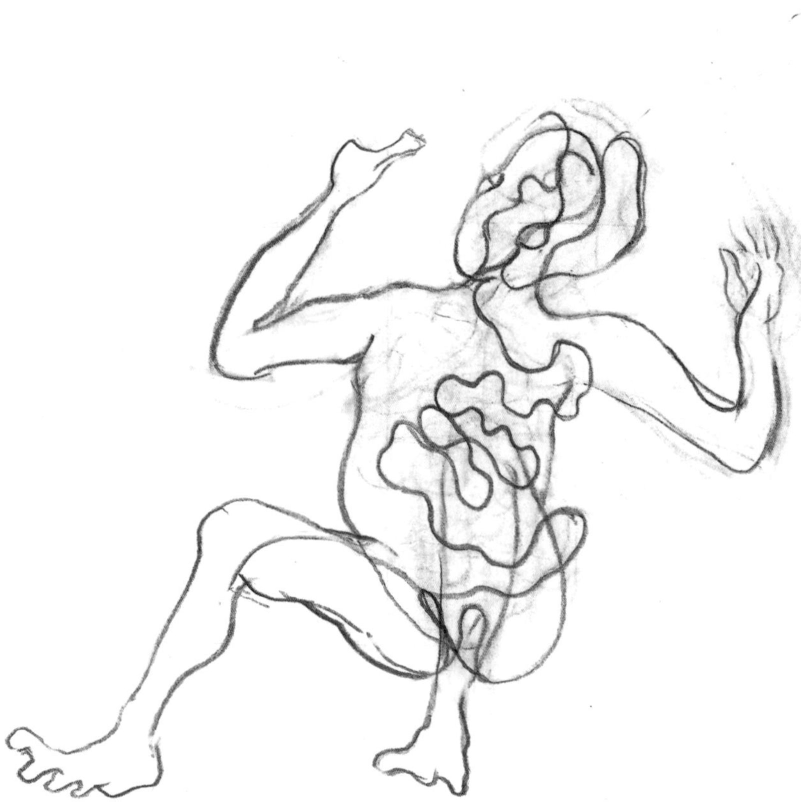

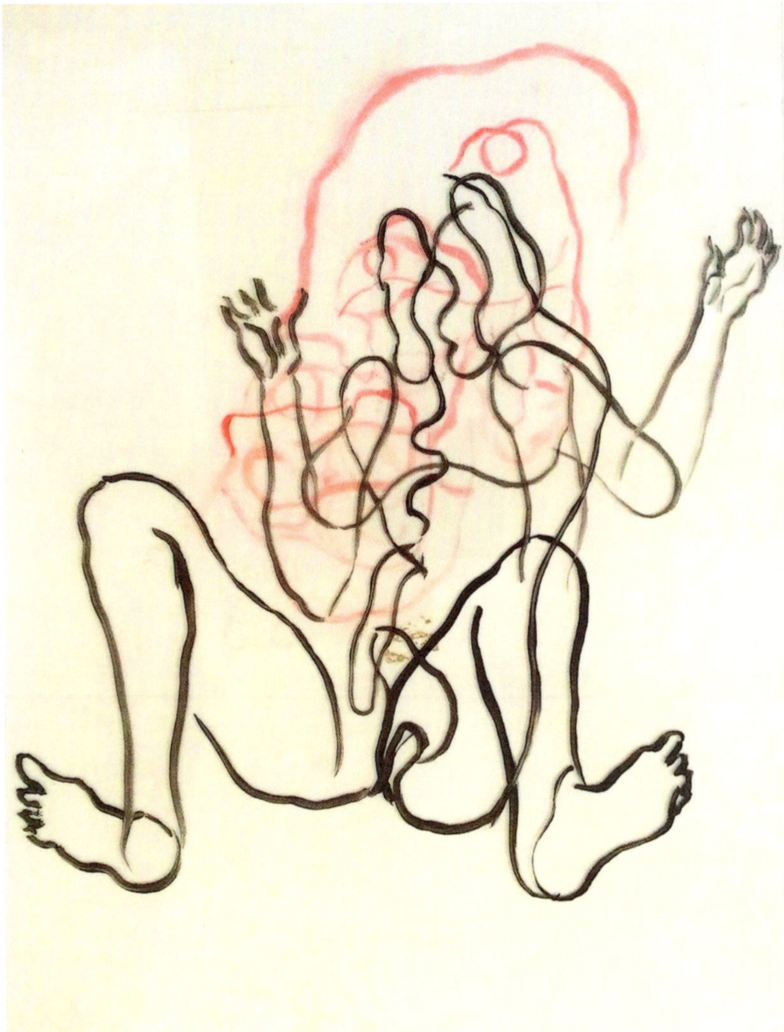

Christine Nippe (C N) im Gespräch mit
Elín Jakobsdóttir (E J)

C N In der Schwartzschen Villa zeigst du zum ersten Mal neue Bilder und einen Film zusammen. Was hat dich dazu bewogen?

E J Es schließt einen Zyklus ab, der im Jahr 2000 in Paris begann. Bei meinen ersten Streifzügen mit Super-8 und 16mm verfolgte ich Gedanken über Malerei mit anderen Mitteln durch das Medium des experimentellen Kinos. In meinem ersten Film mit dem Titel *Sleeping Bag* wirft eine S. 91
Frau einen Leinensack aus einem erhöhten Fenster, der Leinensack erscheint wie ein in einen Abgrund geworfenes Leichentuch. Das war eine Geste in Richtung Malerei – ein Abwerfen des Materials Leinwand. Doch wie auf einem Möbiusband, kehrt sie immer wieder zurück. In dem Film mit dem Titel *In the First Place* kehrt der Leinensack von S. 13–31
Sleeping Bag als Spielobjekt und Vehikel der Verwandlung S. 91
zurück. Die Leinwand wird zu einer aktiv arbeitenden, rezeptiven Oberfläche. Der Sack wird ins Meer geworfen, eine Geste, die ihr Echo in dem Gemälde *Joan and the Whale* S. 43
wiederfindet, wo eine Frau mit ausgestreckten Beinen gefährlich in eine Wassertiefe aus Knochen oder Korallen fällt. So wird die Tasche, die der Schwerkraft überlassen wird, zu einem Vehikel des Begehrens.

C N In der aktuellen Ausstellung interessierst du dich für die Produktion von Bildern und wie sie von unseren inneren Bildern und Erfahrungen gespeist werden. Kannst du das näher beschreiben? Welche Theoretiker*innen waren dabei für dich wichtig?

E J Die Arbeit bewegt sich zwischen der äußeren und der inneren Welt der Wahrnehmung hin und her und testet, wie sich Spuren im Gedächtnis mit einer gegenwärtigen, körperlichen Erfahrung verbinden. Ich habe Theater studiert, bevor ich mich der Malerei widmete. Das Herzstück meiner

Bildsprache ist eine tiefe Kenntnis des Theaters, vor allem über Tadeusz Kantor. In der Theaterschule entdeckte ich die Stücke von Federicon García Lorca, dessen poetische Zeichnungen einen freien Fluss von Ideen und synkretistisches Denken ermöglichen. Die Bilder sind in Schichten aufgebaut, so dass sich nach längerer Zeit allmählich ein Bild herausschält. Dies erfordert ein Loslassen der Kontrolle, um Bilder freizusetzen, die irgendwie an der Schwelle des Bewusstseins schweben. Hier ist das Amorphe der Schlüssel, und die Darstellungen, die ich ins Leben rufe. Beide haben etwas Unheimliches an sich, das zugleich fremd und vertraut ist, wie die Frau, die in
S. 43 *Joan and the Whale* durch den Raum fällt oder die Tasche, die der Junge aus dem Fenster des Hauses wirft. Ich habe sie nie außerhalb der Malerei oder des Films gesehen, aber ich habe sie gefühlt oder geträumt und insofern haben sie die Qualität von Archetypen, die zum ersten Mal in Erscheinung treten.

Ich habe Objekte gemacht, die wie poetische Behälter von Bildern sind, zum Beispiel der Schlafsack aus Leinwand,
S. 88 der eine Fläche zum Malen ist, oder die *Wooden Horsebox*, die auch ein Betrachtungsgerät ist, der zweiseitige Tisch, der durch ein Netz aus geschnittenem Papier in eine Glasscheibe geteilt ist. Diese Objekte, die in den Filmen auftauchen, sind wie Metaphern für den Körper als Gefäß der Bilder.

C N Welchen Unterschied machen die jeweiligen Medien in deiner Arbeit aus, also Malerei, Zeichnung oder Film?

E J Es hat etwas Meteorologisches, wie sie zusammenspielen, wie manche mehr zu verschiedenen Zeiten wachsen. Die Zeichnung kommt zuerst, die erste Markierung, wie die musikalische Notation oder das Schreiben stellt sie die Grundlage her. Es ist erstaunlich in seiner Effizienz, es destilliert und synthetisiert so viel in nur einer Sekunde und synthetisiert so viel in nur ein paar Zeilen. Ich habe sehr alte Zeichnungen, die ich seit Jahrzehnten aufbewahrt habe, wie den Samen von etwas, das darauf wartet, gepflanzt zu werden und ein Baum zu werden. Die Zeichnung enthält die Essenz einer großen Idee. Die Malerei in ihrer Liquidität, ihrer körperlichen

Beteiligung, ihrer Turbulenz, ist unvergleichlich in Bezug auf die Sinnlichkeit, sie ist erschreckend in ihrer Schwierigkeit, sie ist beklemmend durch ihre Geschichte, sie ist ein freudiges Überbleibsel der kindlichen Freiheit. Aus all diesen Gründen ist die Malerei die hohe Berufung, das verborgene Tal, eine Art Goldstandard dessen, was ein Bild sein kann.

Filme entstehen periodisch wie eine Pflanze, die alle paar Jahre unter bestimmten besonderen Bedingungen oder Klimaveränderungen wächst. Wie ich schon sagte, ist Film für mich die Fortsetzung der Malerei mit anderen Mitteln. Ich begann mit dem Film zu experimentieren, als ich in Paris lebte. Ich war mit der Malerei in eine Sackgasse geraten. Ich studierte den nackten Körper in Fragmenten, Hände, Füße, Gliedmaßen. Die Studien waren naturalistisch und die umgebende Leinwand war leer. Ich fand mich in einer Form der Darstellung der Welt des Scheins gefangen. Ich konnte nicht atmen, ich musste raus. Ich lieh mir eine Super-8-Kamera von einem Freund und erlebte die Freiheit, nicht über die unzähligen Möglichkeiten der Malerei nachdenken zu müssen, um die Welt darzustellen.

Ich nahm, was ich in der Theaterschule über Inszenierung gelernt hatte, und begann, Storyboards zu zeichnen. Jede Zeichnung musste bildhaft kommunizieren, indem ich Standbilder kombinierte, die sich als Erzählung lesen. Ich dachte nicht über Ton nach, nur über Bild. Alle meine Filme sind stumm und sie verwenden destillierte Gesten. Bertolt Brechts Verfremdungseffekt hat meine Herangehensweise stark beeinflusst: Nicht-Schauspieler einsetzen, die Erzählung etablieren, verdichten um die Erzählung zu unterlaufen. Ich verwende auch Wiederholungen, die die Erzählstruktur verstärken oder untergraben können und in meinem Fall oft zum Oneirischen tendiert.

C N Du lebst zwischen Glasgow und Berlin. Was ist das Besondere an diesen beiden Orten und wie beeinflussen sie deine künstlerische Arbeit?

E J Beide Städte existieren in den Trümmern weltverändernder historischer Epochen. Sie setzten sich beide mit der Vergangenheit auseinander. Ich habe in Berlin ein Echo meiner Glasgower Nachbarschaft gefunden und verstanden, denn beide teilen eine Mischung aus architektonischer Präsenz des wohlhabenden 19. Jahrhunderts mit dem Post-industriellen mit seinen leerstehenden Grundstücken. Ich habe einen Film S. 89 namens *Horsebox* produziert, den ich in den Straßen rund um die ehemalige AEG-Fabrik, die Behrenshalle, gedreht habe, die von Peter Behrens im Wedding entworfen wurde. Der Film ist eine Hommage an diese Straßen und unterläuft dies mit einem burlesken Register. Ein Holzfahrzeug fährt durch den Film, das einem Pferd ähnelt, einem Kinderwagen, einem Zauberkasten, ähnlich einem Sarg.

Ich las zu dieser Zeit Hannah Arendts Essays. In *Arbeit, Arbeit, Aktion* spricht sie über den dauerhaften Wert des Kunstwerks im Verhältnis zu den für den Konsum produzierten Gegenständen, „In der Sphäre der Fabrikation selbst gibt es nur eine Art von Objekten, denen die unendliche Kette von Mitteln und Zwecken nicht gilt, und das ist das Kunstwerk, das das nutzloseste und zugleich dauerhafteste ist, was Menschenhände herstellen können.‘

C N Die Natur erscheint in deinem aktuellen Film, sei es in Form von blühenden Sommerwiesen oder später als Meer. Was ist dir an ihr wichtig?

E J In Island sieht man wirklich, wie die Natur die Landschaft umgestaltet. Eruptionen schaffen neue Inseln im Meer. Man hört Geschichten über Menschen, die auf einem Gletscher spazieren gehen, durch ein Loch fallen und verschwinden. In dieser mächtigen und gefährlichen Umgebung ist der Mensch verletzlich. Die Natur scheint zufällig, wahllos, nivellierend. Wir konstruieren Geschichten, um damit zurechtzukommen. Ich interessiere mich für die Grenze zwischen dem Erzählten und dem Realen.

C N Vielleicht kannst du auch etwas über Island, deinen Geburtsort, sagen? Was macht Island für dich besonders und inwieweit hat es noch eine Bedeutung für deine künstlerische Arbeit?

E J Der Titel der Ausstellung *In The First Place* bezieht sich auf meine Herkunft aus Island und auch auf mein erstes Medium, die Malerei. Zwei Territorien zu haben, sowohl in Bezug auf das Land als auch auf das Medium bedeutet, ein Doppelleben zu führen. In Island habe ich eine große Familie, mit der ich sehr eng verbunden bin, obwohl ich als Kleinkind nach Schottland gezogen bin. Ich habe mit 15 Jahren einen Sommer lang auf einem Bauernhof in der Nähe von Buðardalur gearbeitet und in Reykjavík hatte ich meine erste Einzelausstellung nach meinem Abschluss an der Glasgow School of Art. Ich würde sagen, dieses Doppelleben sorgt für eine gespaltene Identität, denn man vermisst die Anwesenheit der Menschen und der Landschaft, aber sie bleiben in einer inneren Landschaft bestehen, die man in sich trägt. Ich wollte einen Film machen, der den tatsächlichen Ort beschreibt, also habe ich die Hälfte des Films in Eyrarbakki gedreht, dem ältesten Haus, das noch im Besitz meiner Familie ist.

C N In deinen Filmen geht es oft um die Inszenierung von Raum. Warum fasziniert dich der Raum so sehr?

E J Mehrere der Filme zeigen eine Draufsicht auf einen leeren Tisch oder Boden. Wir können den Produktionsprozess einer Zeichnung beobachten, während der Zeichner uns sein Gedächtnis in Aktion zeigt, während er einen anderen Ort auf einen Grundriss transkribiert. In *Worktable 2* wird S. 95
dieser Grundriss mit Handgesten beschrieben. Das Betrachten des Films offenbart eine Menge Details über Wahrnehmung.

C N In deinen Filmen gibt es oft Momente, die das Unbewusste berühren. Bist du am Konzept von Freud interessiert? Hast du Texte zur Psychoanalyse gelesen?

E J Ich habe Freuds „Die Traumdeutung“ gelesen, nachdem ich gemerkt hatte, wie sehr mich das Thema des Unbewussten interessiert. Drei Jahre lebte ich in Paris mit einem Kreis von Kunsthistorikern, Psychoanalytikern und Künstlern. Sie gaben etwas einen Namen, das ich schon seit einiger Zeit instinktiv verfolgte. Ich las weiter innerhalb des

Freudschen Oeuvres und darüber hinaus zum Beispiel Sami Alis Schriften über die räumliche Darstellung der Psyche in seinem Buch *L'espace imaginaire*.

C N Die kindliche Vorstellungskraft findet in deinen Filmen oft ihren eigenen Ausdruck. Was fasziniert dich daran?

E J Kleine Kinder setzen sich mit ihrer Umwelt in einem transparenten Spiel von Konstruktion und Erfindung auseinander. Sie interessieren sich für Materialität und Berührung, benutzen Objekte und spielen Rollen ohne weltliche Hierarchien, ohne Konsequenzen jenseits der Logik des Spiels. Alles ist eingebunden in das Spiel, den Raum um sie herum als fiktionales Feld. Diese radikale Freiheit ist, glaube ich, eine spätere Grundlage für die Kunst, denn der Spieltrieb, der ludische Instinkt über die Kindheit hinaus fortbesteht, obwohl wir gezwungen sind, ihn zu maskieren oder umzulenken, und imaginäre Ereignisse oder Persönlichkeiten, die sich typischerweise verflüchtigen würden, wenn sich das Spiel eines Kindes erschöpft in der erwachsenen Version des Gedankenspiels bleibt erhalten und kann zum Treibstoff für Kunst werden.

Christine Nippe (C N) in conversation with
Elín Jakobsdóttir (E J)

C N For Schwartzsche Villa you are showing new paintings and a film together for the first time. Can you speak about that?

E J It completes a cycle that began in Paris in 2000. In my first forays with Super8 and 16mm I was pursuing thoughts about painting by other means through the medium of experimental cinema. In my first film entitled *Sleeping Bag*, p. 91 a woman casts a canvas bag from an elevated window, the canvas sack appears like a death shroud thrown into an abyss. This was a gesture towards painting – jettisoning the material canvas. However, as if travelling on a Möbius strip, it keeps returning. In the film entitled *In the First Place*, the canvas pp. 13–31 bag of *Sleeping Bag* reoccurs as an object of play and a vehicle p. 91 of transformation. The canvas becomes an active working receptive surface. The bag is cast into the sea in a gesture which finds its echo in the painting *Joan and the Whale* where a legs p. 43 akimbo woman falls perilously into some aquatic depth of bone or coral. Thus the bag that is jettisoned for gravity to act on it becomes a vehicle of desire.

C N In the current exhibition you are interested in the production of images and how they are fed by our inner images and experience. Can you describe this in more detail? Which theorists were important to you?

E J The work moves back and forth between the outer and the inner world of perception, testing how traces in one's memory connect or re-connect with a present, physical experience. I studied theatre before dedicating myself to painting. At the heart of my pictorial language is a deep knowledge of theatre above all via Tadeusz Kantor. It was at theatre school that I discovered the plays of Federico García Lorca whose poetic drawings allow for a free flow of ideas and syncretic thinking. The paintings are built up in layers so that after a long period of time one image gradually emerges. This requires a letting go of control in order to free images that are somehow hovering on the threshold of consciousness. Here the amorphous is key, and the representations I bring into being have an uncanniness to them, that are both strange and familiar like the woman falling through space in *Joan and* p. 43 *the Whale* or the bag the boy throws from the windows of the house. I never saw these outside of painting or film but I felt them or dreamt them and to this extent they have the quality of archetypes making their first appearance.

I have made objects which are like poetic containers p. 91 of images for example the *Sleeping Bag* made of canvas which p. 88 is a surface for painting or the *Wooden Horsebox* which is p. 92 also a viewing device, the *Two-Sided Table* which is divided by a mesh of cut paper in a glass screen. These objects which appear in the films are like metaphors for the body as a vessel for images.

C N What difference do the respective media make in your work, i.e. painting, drawing or film?

E J There is something meteorological about how they interplay, how some grow more at different times. Drawing comes first, the first mark, like musical notation or writing it lays down an image carried in the mind, it is amazing in its efficiency, it distills and synthesises so much in just a few lines. I have very old drawings that I have kept for decades, like the seed of something waiting to be planted and become a tree, the drawing holds the essence of a big idea.

Painting in its liquidity, its bodily involvement, its turbulence, is incomparable in terms of sensuality, it is terrifying in terms of its difficulty, it is oppressive through its history, it is a joyful remnant of childhood freedom. For all these reasons, painting is the high calling, the hidden valley, a kind of gold standard of what an image can be. Films happen periodically like a plant that flowers every couple of years under some special conditions or change in climate. As I said earlier, film for me is the continuation of painting by other means. I began experimenting with film while living in Paris. I had reached an impasse with painting. I was studying the naked body in fragments, hands, feet, limbs. The studies were naturalistic and the surrounding canvas was blank. I found myself stuck in a form of representation of the world of appearance. I couldn't breathe, I had to get out. I borrowed a Super8 camera from a friend and experienced the freedom of not having to think about the myriad of possibilities within painting for depicting the world. I took what I had learned from theatre school about staging and began to draw storyboards. Each drawing had to communicate pictorially combining still images that read as narrative. I didn't think about sound, just about picture. All my films are silent, and they use distilled gestures. Bertolt Brecht's alienation effect (Verfremdungseffekt) has hugely influenced my approach; using non actors, establishing, condensing and subverting the narrative. I also use repetition which can reinforce or undermine the narrative structure and in my case often tends towards the oneiric.

C N You live between Glasgow and Berlin. What is special about these two places and how do they influence your artistic work?

E J Both cities exist in the rubble of world changing historical periods. They are both coming to terms with the past. I found an echo of my Glasgow neighbourhood in Berlin and understood it since both share a mixture of the architectural presence of the prosperous 19th Century with the post-industrial and its vacant grounds. I made a film called *Horsebox* p. 89 which I shot in the streets around the former AEG factory, the Behrenshalle, designed by Peter Behrens in Wedding. The film pays tribute to those streets and then undermines this with a burlesque register. A wooden vehicle passes through the film resembling a horse, a child's pram, a magician's sawing box, a coffin. I was reading Hannah Arendt's essays at the time. In *Labor, Work, Action* she talks about the durable value of the artwork in relation to objects produced for consumption, 'In the sphere of fabrication itself, there is only one kind of object to which the unending chain of means and ends does not apply, and this is the work of art, the most useless and, at the same time, the most durable thing human hands can produce.'

C N Nature appears in your current film, be it in the form of flowering summer meadows or later as the sea. What is important to you about it?

E J In Iceland you really see how nature transforms the landscape. Eruptions create new islands in the sea. You hear stories about people who go walking on a glacier, fall through a hole and disappear. Within this powerful and dangerous environment human beings are vulnerable. Nature seems random, indiscriminate, levelling. We construct stories to come to terms with it. I'm interested in the edge between the narrative and the real.

C N Perhaps you could also say something about Iceland, your birthplace? What makes Iceland special for you and to what extent does it still have a meaning for your artistic work?

pp. 13–31

E J The title of the exhibition *In The First Place* refers to my origins in Iceland and also my first medium which is painting. Having two territories both in terms of country and of medium means having a double life. In Iceland, I have a large family with whom I have close ties despite leaving to live in Scotland when I was an infant. Iceland provided many formative experiences; I worked for a summer on a farm near Buðardalur when I was 15 and it was in Reykjavík that I had my first solo exhibition after graduating from Glasgow School of Art. I would say this double life makes for a split identity since you miss the presence of the people and the landscape but they persist within an inner landscape that you carry inside you. I wanted to make a film that describes the actual place, so I shot half of it in Eyrarbakki which is the oldest house still in my family's possession.

C N Your films are often about the production of space. Why does space fascinate you so much?

E J Several of the films show an overhead shot of a blank table or floor. We can watch the progress of a drawing captured on film while the drawer reveals to us his memory in action as he transcribes another place onto a ground plan. In *Worktable 2* this ground plan is described using hand gestures. p. 95 It is traced using vision and a corporeal awareness of space. Watching it on film reveals a lot of detail about perception.

C N There are often moments in your films that touch on the unconscious. Are you interested in this concept of Freud? Have you studied psychoanalysis?

E J I read Freud's *The Interpretation of Dreams* after coming to realise how deeply I was interested in the subject of the unconscious. Three years living in Paris with a circle of friends that included art historians, psychoanalysts and artists gave a name to something I had been pursuing instinctively for some time. I read further within the Freud oeuvre and beyond for example, Sami Ali's writings concerning the spacial representation of the psyche in his book *L'espace imaginaire*.

C N The childlike imagination often finds its own expression in your films. What fascinates you about it?

E J Young children engage with their environment in a transparent game of construction and invention. They are interested in materiality and touch, using objects and playing roles without worldly hierarchical judgement, with no consequences beyond the logic of play. Everything is taken up in the game of building the space around them as a fictional field. It is this radical freedom, I believe, that is a later basis for art since the ludic instinct continues beyond childhood although we are obliged to mask it or redirect it, and imaginary events or personalities that would typically evaporate when play is exhausted by a child are retained in the adult version of mind playfulness becoming fuel for art making.

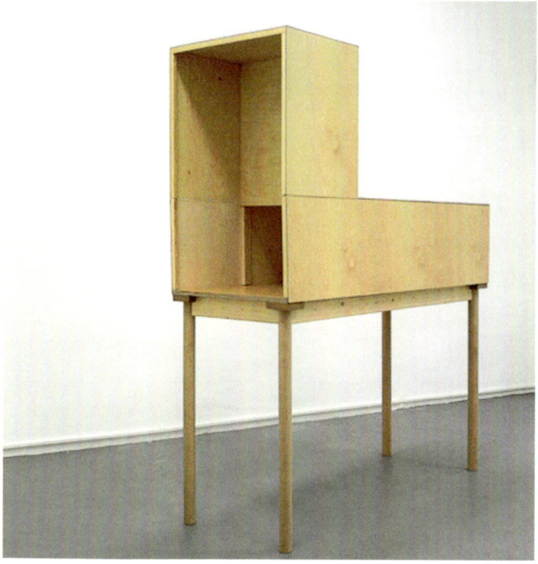

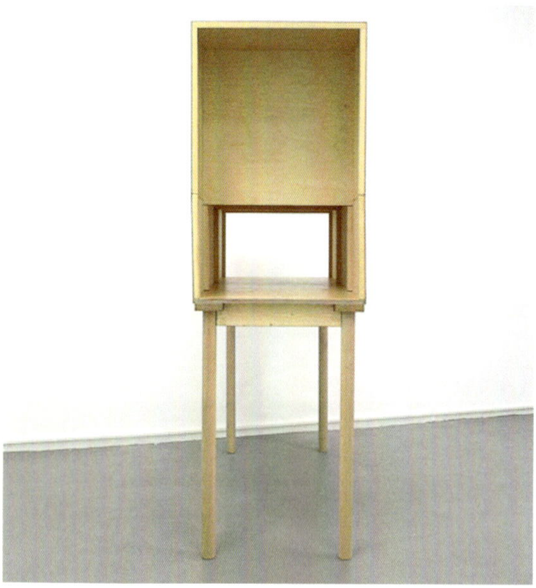

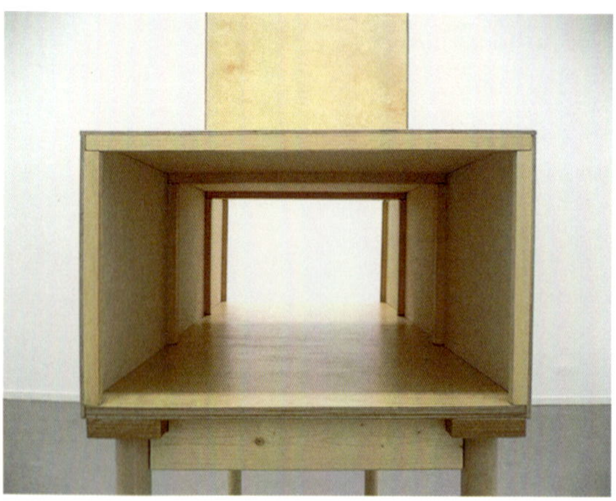

Wooden Horsebox
Holz
birch plywood, beechwood
150 × 60 × 180 cm
2007

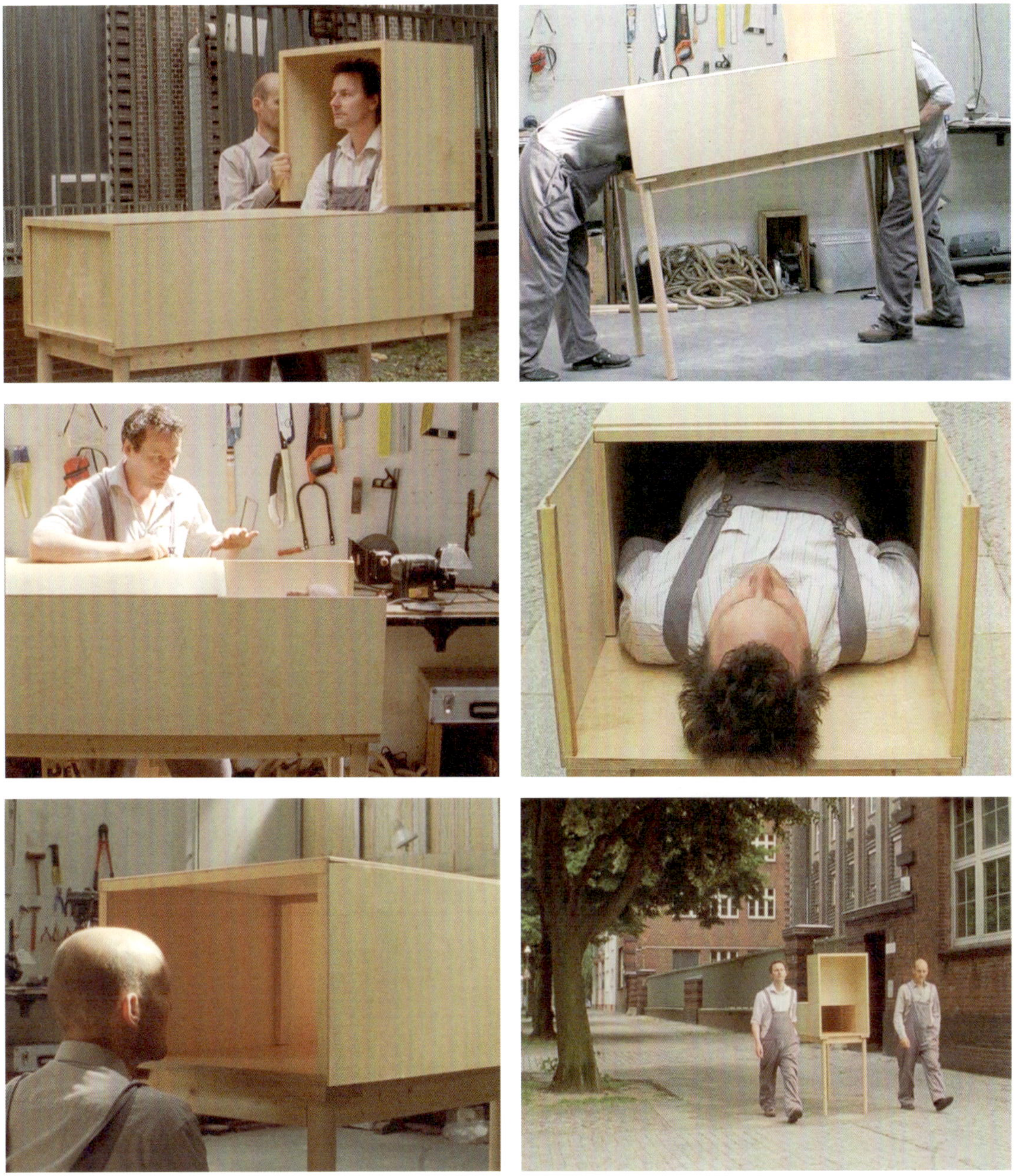

Horsebox
16mm-Film zu DVD transferiert
16mm film transferred to DVD
11 minutes, silent
2009

Sleeping Bag
Super-8-Film zu DVD transferiert
Super8 film transferred to DVD
10 minutes, silent
2001

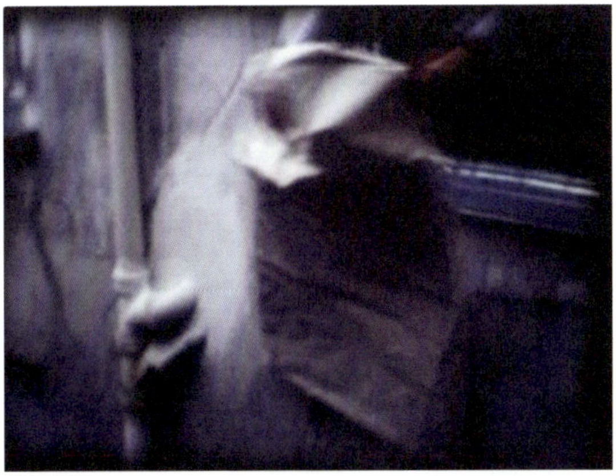
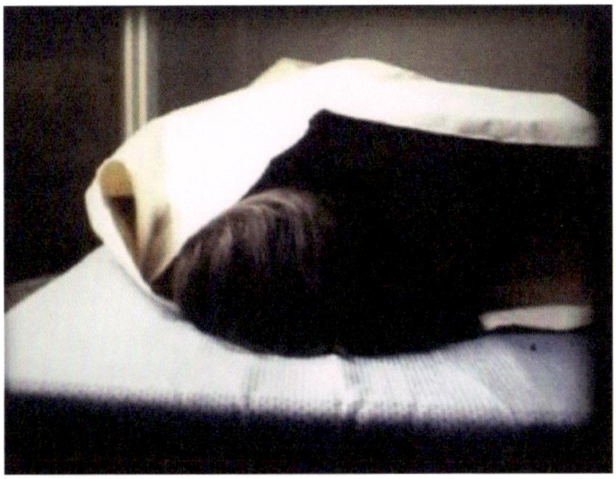
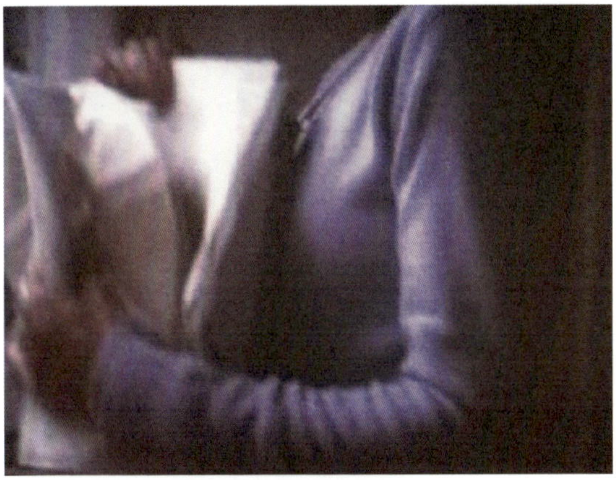
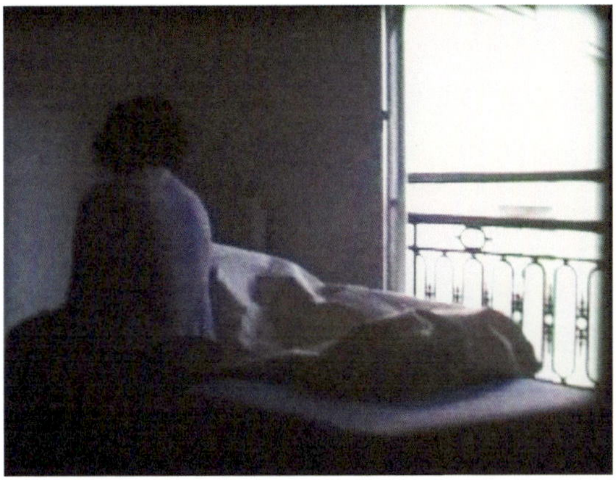
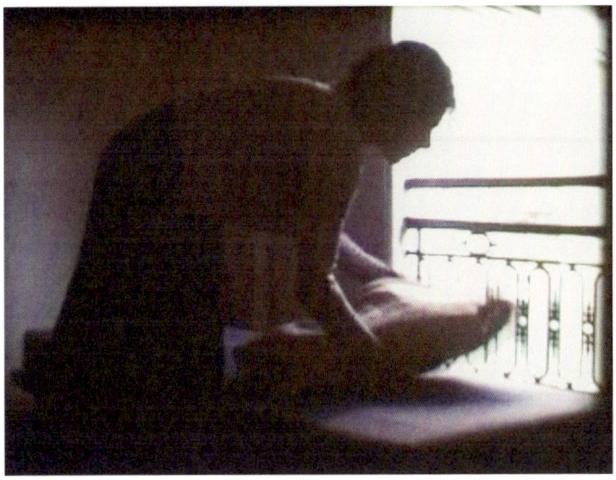

Two-Sided Table
Holz, Glas, Papier
wood, glass, paper
120 × 60 × 140 cm
2008

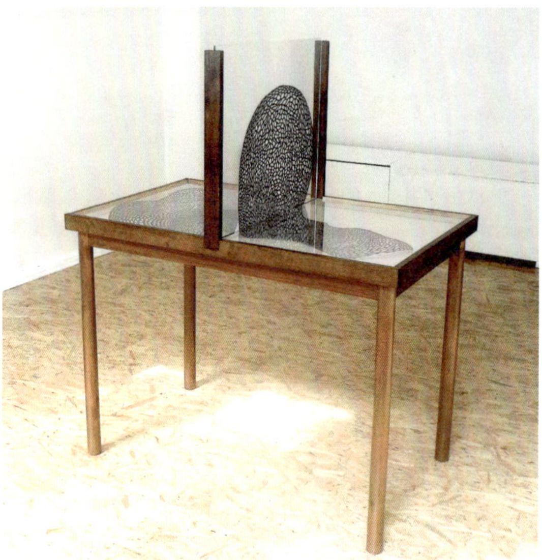

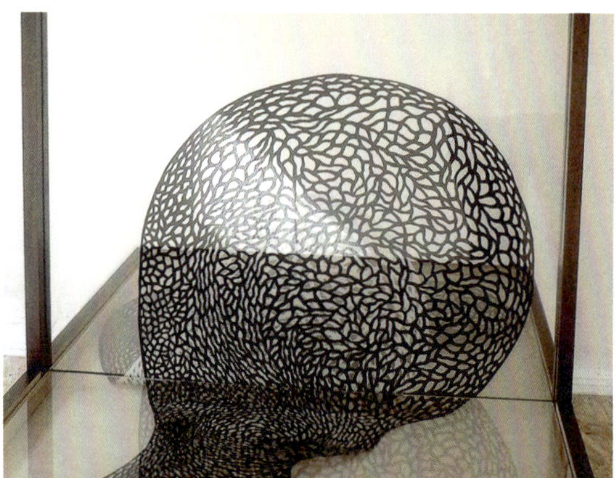

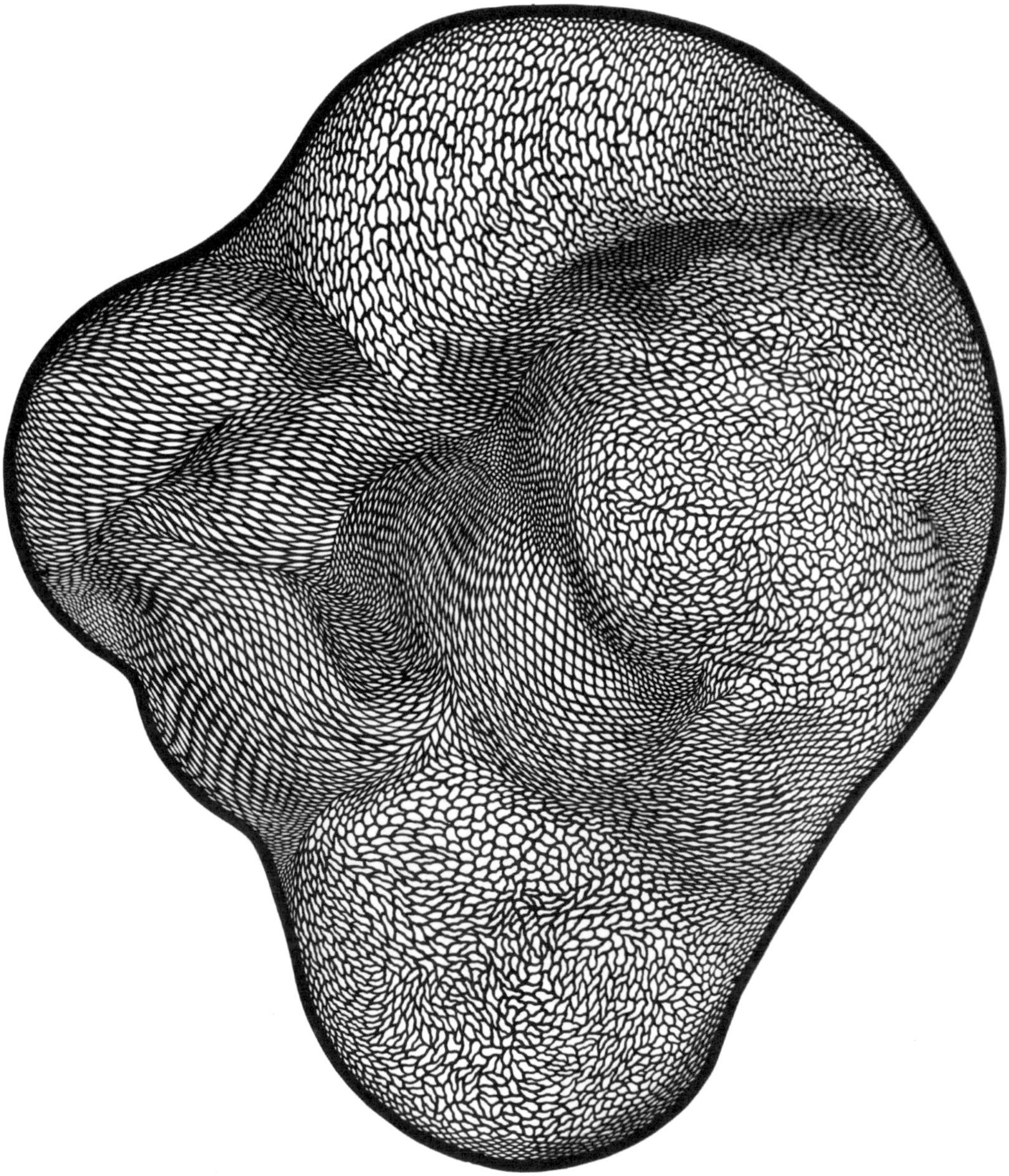

Black Paper Cut-Out No. 2
Papier, Gouache
paper, gouache
150 × 165 cm
2018

Worktable 1
Super-8-Film zu DVD transferiert
Super8 film transferred to DVD
12 minutes, silent
2003

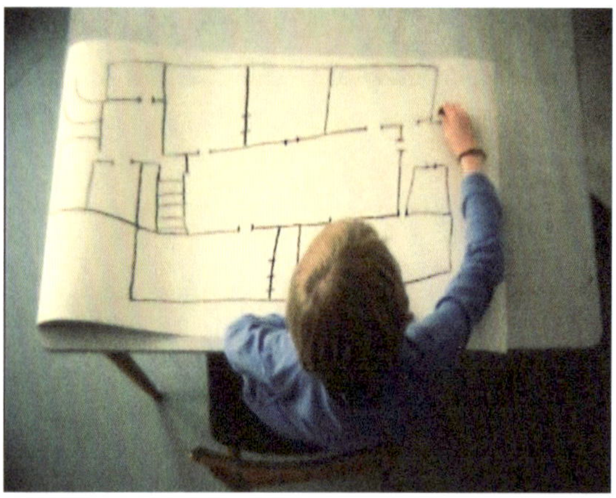

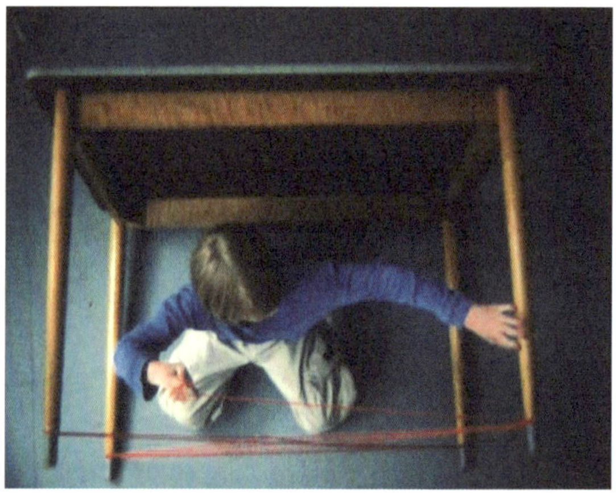

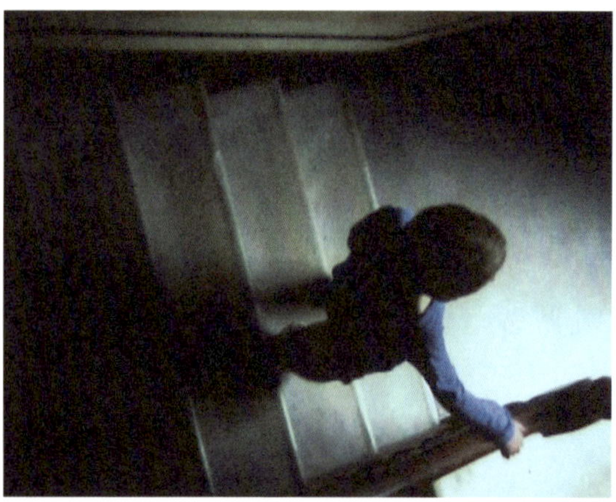

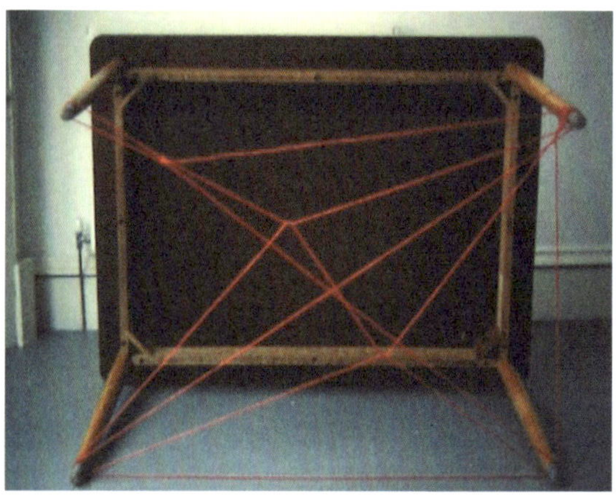

Worktable 2
Super-8-Film zu DVD transferiert
Super8 film transferred to DVD
12 minutes, silent
2009

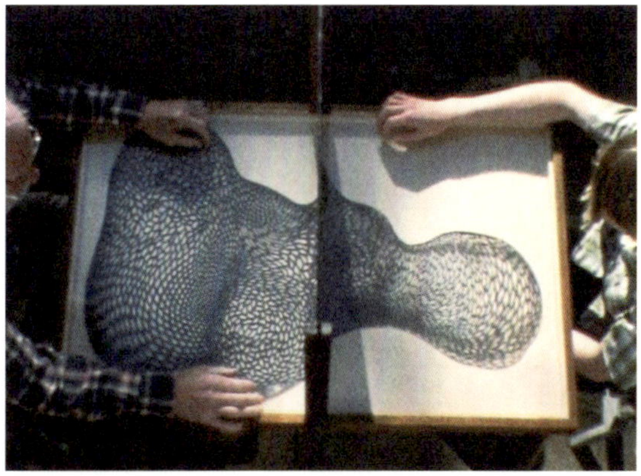

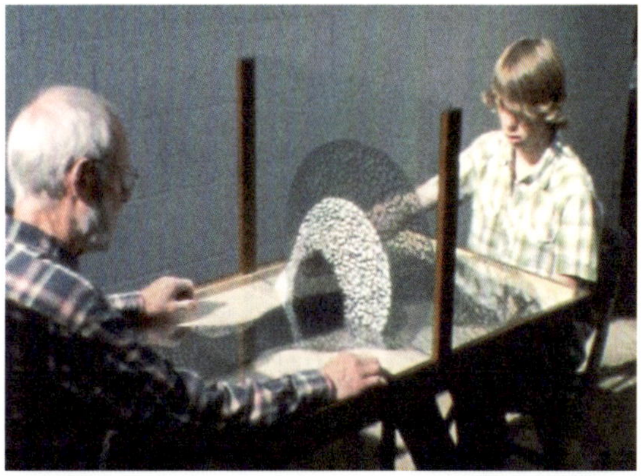

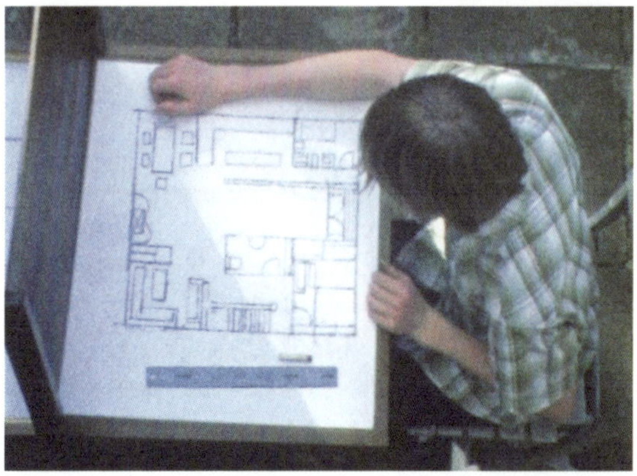

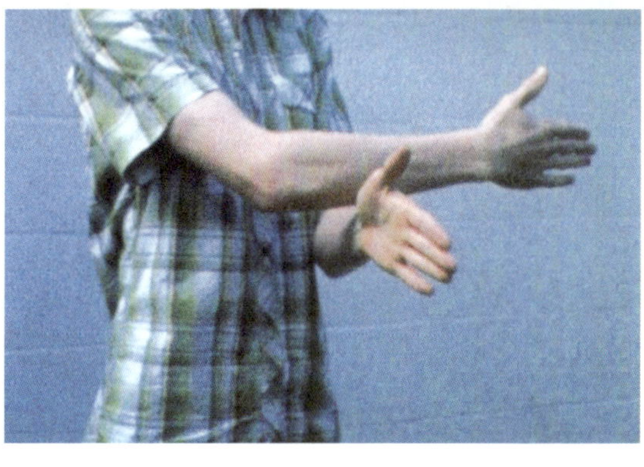

Diese Publikation erscheint anlässlich der Ausstellung/
This publication is released to accompany the exhibition
Elín Jakobsdóttir „In the First Place"
04.06.–31.10.2021
Schwartzsche Villa
Grunewaldstraße 55
12165 Berlin-Steglitz

Herausgegeben von/
Edited by
Christine Nippe
Bezirksamt Steglitz-Zehlendorf von Berlin
Amt für Weiterbildung und Kultur
Fachbereich Kultur
Grunewaldstraße 3
12165 Berlin
Tel +49 (0)30 90299-2212
www.kultur-steglitz-zehlendorf.de

Leitung der Abteilung/
Head of Department
Frank Mückisch

Leitung des Fachbereichs Kultur/
Head of the Cultural Department
Dr. Brigitte Hausmann

Redaktion/Editorial staff
Elín Jakobsdóttir
& Christine Nippe

Gestaltung/Design
Wolfgang Hückel

Lektorat/Copyediting
Anja Braun

Übersetzungen/Translations
Michael Wetzel

Projektmanagement/
Project Management
Kerber Verlag, Lydia Fuchs

Herstellung/Production
Kerber Verlag, Jens Bartneck

Gesamtherstellung/
Printed and published by
Kerber Verlag
Windelsbleicher Str. 166–170
33659 Bielefeld
Germany
+49 521 950 08 10
+49 521 950 08 88 (F)
info@kerberverlag.com
kerberverlag.com

Kerber Publikationen werden weltweit vertrieben/
Kerber publications are distributed worldwide

ACC Art Books
Sandy Lane
Old Martlesham
Woodbridge, IP12 4SD
UK
+44 1394 38 99 50
+44 1394 38 99 99 (F)
accartbooks.com
uksales@accartbooks.com

Artbook | D.A.P.
75 Broad Street, Suite 630
New York, NY 10004
USA
+1 212 627 19 99
+1 212 627 94 84 (F)
artbook.com
orders@dapinc.com

AVA Verlagsauslieferung AG
Centralweg 16
8910 Affoltern am Albis
Switzerland
+41 44 762 42 50
+41 44 762 42 10 (F)
avainfo@ava.ch

Zeitfracht GmbH
Verlagsauslieferung
kerber-verlag@knv-zeitfracht.de

Die Deutsche Nationalbibliothek verzeichnet diese Publikation in der Deutschen Nationalbibliografie: dnb.de./
The Deutsche Nationalbibliothek lists this publication in the Deutsche Nationalbibliografie: dnb.de.

Gefördert aus Mitteln des Ausstellungsfonds für die Kommunalen Galerien der Berliner Bezirke und des Bezirkskulturfonds.
The project is generously supported by the Ausstellungsfonds für die Kommunalen Galerien der Berliner Bezirke and the Bezirkskulturfonds.

Dank/Acknowledgements

Mark Sadler
The Guardians of Læknishúsið, Eyrarbakki, Iceland
The Hope Scott Trust, Edinburgh, Scotland

ISBN 978-3-7356-0797-3

www.kerberverlag.com
Printed in Germany